Lamb

JANE BODIE

with lyrics by
MARK SEYMOUR

Currency Press,
Sydney

RED
STITCH

THE
ACTORS'
THEATRE

CURRENCY THEATRE SERIES

First published in 2018
by Currency Press Pty Ltd,
PO Box 2287, Strawberry Hills, NSW, 2012, Australia
enquiries@currency.com.au
www.currency.com.au
in association with Red Stitch Actors' Theatre
Reprinted 2021

For copies of Mark Seymour's sheet music written for *Lamb*, please contact
Mushroom Music, 9 Dundas Lane, Albert Park VIC 3206, Australia;
ph: +61 3 9690 3399; email: info@mushroommusic.com
Typeset by Dean Nottle for Currency Press.
Front cover shows (from left to right) Brigid Gallacher, Simon Maiden, Emily
Goddard (Photographer Robert Blackburn).

Currency Press acknowledges the Traditional Owners of the Country on which
we live and work. We pay our respects to all Aboriginal and Torres Strait
Islander Elders, past and present.

A catalogue record for this
book is available from the
National Library of Australia

Contents

For Annie, Daniel and George.

'A lone sheep, until it no longer has strength to stand, will seek to return to its flock.'

The Woolgrower's Companion, 1906

Thanks for *Lamb*.

Thank you to David and Debbie Shaffer Bain, for time at their beautiful farm and home, for their warmth and generosity, and tales of real life and work on a sheep farm. I hope I've got some small part of it right.

Thanks to Iain Sinclair, for his vast dramaturgical brain and heart, all through this process, and to Tim at PWA for his unwavering support and friendship. To Julian M, for smarts, delicacy and clarity, always. And to Mari Lourey, for reading early drafts and her lived country knowledge and true playwright's soul.

Thank you, Ella, for all you give, for your endless commitment and nurture, to this and other new work; to Mark S, for his beautiful songs, at the heart of the play; and to our sublime and gifted cast, for this first outing: Brigid, Simon and Emily. My thanks must also go to the original cast of the play in development, Eva, Paul and Sarah, who gave much.

And to John, thank you, for everything else.

JB

Lamb was first produced by Red Stitch Actors' Theatre and presented, in association with Playwriting Australia, in Melbourne on 13 November 2018 with the following cast:

PATRICK / FRANK	Simon Maiden
ANNIE / MARY	Brigid Gallacher
KATHLEEN	Emily Goddard

Director, Julian Meyrick
Dramaturgs, Iain Sinclair, Ella Caldwell
Songwriter, Mark Seymour
Set & Costume Designer, Greg Clarke
Lighting Designer, Efterpi Soropos
Sound Designer, Justin Gardam
Stage Manager, Alysha Watt
Assistant Stage Manager, Zsuzsa Gaynor Mihaly
Production Trainee, Millie Spencer

This project has been assisted by the Australian government through the Department of Communication and the Arts' Catalyst—Australian Arts and Culture Fund. This play was developed through Red Stitch's INK writing program, proudly supported by: Cybec Foundation, Lyngala Foundation, Malcolm Robertson Foundation, City of Port Phillip, Copyright Australia, and the Seaborn, Broughton & Walford Foundation.

playwriting
australia

CHARACTERS

PATRICK / FRANK, mid 30s

ANNIE / MARY, 20s

KATHLEEN, late 30s, early 40s

SETTING

An old-style country pub. A small bar to one side, a pub TV (the style of the TV and content playing to show/denote the year or era). A door leading to a visible bathroom sink (the unmodernised pub toilet). Mugs, medals, photos of the past and paraphernalia line the walls. The pub should have a small stage area, nothing fancy—bingo and live, mostly local, music is performed here.

The other side of the stage is a farm kitchen. This can be bare in the most part, something lonely about it—though it should have part of the old original flooring, a comfortable old chair, kitchen table and fridge. Possibly a fireplace and window. The sense of the farm outside and a small patch of earth, representing the land outside, ground and sky, for both pub and house.

PUNCTUATION RULES

A slash (/) indicates an interruption point in the dialogue.

An ellipsis (…) indicates a trailing-off of dialogue.

No punctuation at the end of a line of dialogue indicates a direct cutting-off, an unfinished thought, or an inability to complete the sentence.

This play went to press before the end of rehearsals and may differ from the play as performed.

ACT ONE

SCENE ONE

The pub. The present.

Late afternoon. The end of a wake that has taken place. Sad platters of half-eaten food litter the place, lamb rissoles et cetera.

PATRICK *steps onto the small pub stage and takes the microphone. He's wearing a flannelette shirt and a dark suit jacket, that looks somehow wrong on him. He looks out to the empty room, to us.*

PATRICK: I'd like to … to thank you all, for coming today. For Mary … Mum.

>Though … not sure she'd have approved of this.

>*Beat.*

And to be honest, she'd have fucking hated the food.

>*He laughs, but it's sad. He stares ahead a little, unsure what to say, speechless a moment. Then he picks up the guitar, a little unsteady, from grief or booze, or both.*

But this is for her.

>*He begins to play 'Book of Lies'. He plays the first verse as an intro, without singing. He then begins the first verse, quietly.*

SONG: 'BOOK OF LIES'

PATRICK: [*singing*] Tell me a story
>>From your book of lies
>>Make it all about you
>>Everyone's gotta name their price
>>You got mine covered too
>>You left a trail of broken bread
>>'Cross the old battle ground
>>Behind the veil of the living and the dead
>>You wrote your secrets down.

ANNIE *enters from the toilet and stops when she sees* PATRICK *singing. She wears a vintage dress, something from the mid seventies—it suits her.*

PATRICK *keeps singing, not seeing her, involved in the song now, his eyes closed.*

> Now the last train is leaving now
> The last song bird has flown
> At the call to prayer
> I'll be standing there
> When they roll away the stone.

PATRICK *falters, as if no longer able to go on.* ANNIE *now starts the next verse, alone.*

ANNIE: Lead me on
> Give me words to believe
> Now you got my attention
> Give it up
> It was always a game
> Something you forgot to mention.

> When the work is done
> And the last word is read
> And the last light fades from your eyes
> The time will come
> To take back what you said
> When the last holy arrow flies.

And then they sing together.

PATRICK and ANNIE: But the children cried
> When they lost their way
> But they followed the bread back home
> Now the cost of love has captured you
> Now they're rolling back the stone.

Growing in energy and harmony, they are born to sing together, whether they like it or not.

> Now the stars shine and the seed grows tall
> Can't you hear the lyrebird sing?

Feel the burn as the shot goes down
Stain movin' under your skin
Everyone's got a name in this town
They all know what you've done
Every caress, every turn of the screw
As the little lambs played in the sun.

And the words rise up and they burn for you
Now you've taken the road back home
The memory will hang like glue
Now we're rollin' back the stone.

Now the last train is leaving now
The last song bird has flown
Hear the call to prayer—

PATRICK *stops singing, playing.* ANNIE *is left singing the final two lines alone.*

ANNIE: I'll be standing there
        When they roll away [the stone.]

ANNIE *doesn't sing the last two words of the chorus.*

PATRICK *now stares at* ANNIE, *who stands there a moment.*

ANNIE: [*spoken*] Who you singing to?

He puts down the guitar.

PATRICK: Thought you'd left.
ANNIE: Nope, still here.
PATRICK: Unlike everybody else.

Beat.

ANNIE: I wouldn't have left without saying goodbye.

Beat.

It's beautiful, Patrick, your
PATRICK: It's over.

He steps off the stage, comes to the bar. He grabs a beer.

ANNIE: Thought maybe, people would have stuck around.
PATRICK: For what?

ANNIE: Not the food, obviously.

PATRICK: Na. They all went home.

ANNIE: Like sheep.

She smiles.

Except for you.

PATRICK: Molly left me the keys.

ANNIE: She must have been drunker than I thought.

He raises his beer—a cheers.

PATRICK: Let's just say, it came to a, natural end.

Beat.

ANNIE: Kat should have been here today.

PATRICK: [*a dig*] People deal with grief in different ways. And she doesn't like being called Kat anymore.

ANNIE: Should she be left alone? I mean, today

PATRICK: She's not alone. She's got three thousand sheep to keep her company.

Beat.

Molly took her round some food. She'll stay with her, till I'm back.

ANNIE: [*nodding*] When will that be?

PATRICK: Right now [*holding up his beer*] say it'd be a while away.

She nods—not a leg to stand on. He swigs.

ANNIE *sits down—she's tired.*

Thought you were heading off.

You don't have to stay around, not now.

He swigs.

ANNIE: Train's been cancelled.

Beat.

Until Monday.

She goes to look at her phone.

PATRICK: [*smiling*] Google that, did ya?

He swigs, ribbing her. She looks at him, doesn't rise to it.

ANNIE: There's a replacement bus service on apparently, in

She looks at her phone.

Actually I'm not sure when it's … if it's …

PATRICK *laughs to himself.*

PATRICK: Can't get you to come back for five years, now we can't get rid of ya. *Bonza.*

ANNIE: Why d'you have to be so … clichéd? I mean even your … that shirt is

PATRICK: Never gets old, this look. Not round here.

He offers her a beer, she shakes her head.

She puts her phone away, checks in her bag.

Lost your smokes?

She stops looking in her bag.

So, you still pissed off about me moving into your room?

ANNIE: It's not my … This is what I get like, after three days without a real coffee.

PATRICK: You should have said. Could have got some in.

Place down the road now, does soy lattes. Place is changing.

ANNIE: [*looking around at the pub*] Not this place.

PATRICK: And it's two days, two days you been here. And it was always your room, Annie, ever since you wangled it, aged eleven

ANNIE: [*correcting him*] Wrangled.

And I didn't … we tossed for it. We tossed, Patrick, fair and square.

PATRICK: Yeah, and I won. You cried for two days and then Dad said you should have it.

ANNIE: I was having bad dreams. I wanted a room up the back, with a, view.

PATRICK: And you couldn't hear the shearing from there, only room in the house.

She stops, looks at him, goes to wipe at a fly, stops herself.

I didn't move into it till after she'd gone. She'd kept it exactly as you left it.

ANNIE: Mum didn't like not to be in control.

PATRICK: Well, she lost that, she fucking well and truly lost that, the last year, two.

Anger in this. ANNIE *gulps, in pain. Then from behind the bar,* PATRICK *takes out a small paper plate. He holds it out. It's a mezze platter, vegetarian.*

Molly put this behind the bar for you before. Told her you probably wouldn't be able to eat much of the other stuff.

ANNIE: Good old Molly.

PATRICK: It was me went and got it for ya.

She doesn't take it.

ANNIE: Thanks.

PATRICK: Felafels, some hummus, aioli. From the place down the road. Didn't get a chance to tell you, what with

She reaches out and takes it.

ANNIE: Thank you.

PATRICK: Chickpea flour, apparently.

She looks down at it.

ANNIE: I thought, for a minute. Thought it was …

PATRICK: Aussie rissoles.

ANNIE: Yeah.

She laughs, relieved.

Yes.

Beat.

PATRICK: A … is for …

ANNIE: What?

PATRICK: *A*, is for

ANNIE: Oh no, I'm not doing this.

PATRICK: A is for *Aussie rissoles.*

B, is for …

ANNIE: Patrick, I'm not

PATRICK: Told you, you've gone soft.

Beat.

ANNIE: [*coolly*] Backstrap.

He grins.

Beat.

PATRICK: Chops.

ANNIE: Bit obvious

She takes his beer off the bar, swigs at it.

He gets another beer.

PATRICK: Chermoula.

ANNIE: Better. Though it's not strictly … And when did you bloody have chermoula?

PATRICK: … D.

ANNIE: *Where* did you / have

PATRICK: It's D now.

ANNIE: Yeah I *know*. I know. [*Thinking*] Just give me a …

PATRICK: There isn't one.

ANNIE: What?

PATRICK: There isn't a lamb dish, with a D.

ANNIE: What? Of course there bloody—

She swigs.

Just give me a second.

He gives her a beat.

PATRICK: There isn't one. Mum said there wasn't one, and she'd know

ANNIE: Of course she would. D, D … fucking / *D*

PATRICK: E. Just move on to E, unless you can't

ANNIE: Enchiladas, lamb enchiladas!

She points, in victory. He smiles, a real one this time.

PATRICK: Fajitas. Lamb fucking fajitas. Take that, city girl.

ANNIE: I don't want to do this actually

PATRICK: Oh … *come on*. Dig a little / deeper

ANNIE: No, I really / don't

PATRICK: Hey, I bought a vego platter, day of Mum's funeral, whole town'll be talking about it / now.

ANNIE: I'm not playing this game, *okay*!

Beat.

She breathes. A moment.

PATRICK: Stupid bloody game anyway.

Beat.

ANNIE: You went through her stuff, Patrick, without me, her private /
    stuff.

PATRICK: It was just a book full of scribbles, clippings, thing she used
    all the time.

    Wasn't sure if you'd come at all.

ANNIE: You still should have waited.

PATRICK: I thought it was her *recipe* folder, Annie.

ANNIE: And she knew you hated cooking.

PATRICK: I hated *her* cooking.

ANNIE: Wasn't really cooking, was it? No love lost there.

PATRICK: Not the cuisine you'd be used to, no. Pop down the local pop-
    up boutique beer place in an Uber.

    No, fair enough, that was a bit clichéd. Sorry.

    Beat.

    ANNIE *goes to walk towards him, to touch him. He looks frightened.*

    She hated lamb.

ANNIE: [*stopping*] … What?

PATRICK: Mum, she hated the smell of it, the taste. Spent two years
    having to cook the stuff, come up with new ways of using meat every
    day, night, and the smell of the … flesh, made her sick to her stomach,
    gave her nightmares.

ANNIE: … Shit.

PATRICK: Reckon she'd lived in another time she'd have been a vegetarian
    too.

ANNIE: Yeah, and Dad would have had therapy, anger management.

PATRICK: Na, he wouldn't have.

    Beat.

    *He does something, behind the bar—opens a fridge, gets another
    beer?*

ANNIE: I'm glad it was here. I think, Mum would have liked it. Some of
    it.

    Though not the food obviously.

    A sad smile between them both.

    I didn't know you wrote songs.

PATRICK: Yeah, well I didn't know you knew that song.

Beat.

ANNIE: I listened to the recording you made.

I haven't stopped listening to it. The songs are good, Patrick, I mean, they're really good.

Beat.

Maybe, we could … I could, help you. With my profile, contacts

PATRICK: Na, y'alright.

Wouldn't want to get my hopes up.

As you're leaving.

He swigs.

ANNIE: Patrick …

But her phone buzzes in her pocket, distracting her. She reaches for it, pulls it out, looks at it.

It's … my ride's here.

PATRICK: Bus driver got your number?

ANNIE: I … booked an Uber. To the next town, more trains will be running from there.

He nods—might have guessed.

I didn't know you could sing like that.

PATRICK But we all knew you could.

Pause.

Between them, years of pain, not ready to go there yet.

Her dress, it looks good on ya.

ANNIE: Say goodbye to Kat, Kathleen, for me.

She readies to leave.

PATRICK: You should know, there's been an offer on the farm.

ANNIE: But … you said, that no-one round here could afford it.

PATRICK: They're not from round here. It's the land they want.

ANNIE: For what?

PATRICK: Whatever they want, if they can pay the asking price.

ANNIE: What's our asking price?

PATRICK: My asking price, you mean?

A car horn.

Beat.

ANNIE: When did you write them, the songs?

He doesn't give her an answer, won't.

The car horn sounds again, louder this time, impatient.

I have to

She motions to outside, the car waiting.

PATRICK: Yeah.

He holds up his hand, a full stop to the conversation and a goodbye.

She looks at him, then leaves.

He finishes his beer, then looks down to see that she has left her untouched platter. He picks it up. He stands up, bins it, looks around the place, as the lights fade.

SCENE TWO

The farm kitchen. The night before.

It's the middle of the night. KATHLEEN *is up, standing at the kitchen table. She is humming 'The Whole World is Dreaming' to herself. She's dressed in a nightgown, something old-fashioned.*

There is a small light on and a recipe folder is open on the table, which is covered in opened jars, packets of flour spilling out, bowls, eggs and lamb cutlets. The recipe folder is open from the back, but KATHLEEN *has stopped cooking.*

ANNIE *enters, dressed in a long T-shirt, barefoot, her hair loose. She surveys the scene.*

ANNIE: Shit.

KATHLEEN *looks up, but doesn't move. A moment.*

Thought you were asleep.

Beat.

KATHLEEN: I thought you were Mum.

ANNIE *sits down at the table, opposite* KATHLEEN *and the mess.* KATHLEEN *looks down at the mess.*

ANNIE: Sorry I missed you earlier. I tried waiting up, you must have got
   home late.

KATHLEEN: You shouldn't say that.

ANNIE: What?

KATHLEEN: The S word.

   Beat.

ANNIE: [*with love*] Hey, Kat.

KATHLEEN: Hey, Possum.

ANNIE: [*laughing*] What?

KATHLEEN: You say, 'Hey, *Possum*'.

ANNIE: Is that what … what Mum used / to

KATHLEEN: I'm not supposed to be in the kitchen on my own.

   She looks at ANNIE. *A moment*

Where are you slippers, Annie?

ANNIE: I … must have forgot to pack them.

   Beat.

KATHLEEN: Did you come down for a cigarette?

ANNIE: No.

KATHLEEN: I can't sleep.

ANNIE: [*nodding*] Well, we can stay up together, for a bit.

   Beat.

KATHLEEN: I was cooking

ANNIE: Cooking up a storm.

KATHLEEN: I've made a bit of a mess.

ANNIE: That's okay.

KATHLEEN: But you're supposed to clean up as you go, so it's less work
   later.

ANNIE: I won't tell.

   KATHLEEN *doesn't move.*

What are you making then, other than a mess?

KATHLEEN: Finger food.

ANNIE: [*in a silly voice*] Better watch your fingers then.

   KATHLEEN *doesn't get the joke.*

Proper midnight feast, eh, always wanted one of those.

KATHLEEN: No, it's what people have, Annie. That and …

> *It's clear she can't think of the word.*

I was doing cutlets. Crumbed cutlets.

ANNIE: Fancy.

KATHLEEN: From the freezer. I was using Mum's book.

ANNIE: Which book?

> *Beat.*

KATHLEEN: I'm not supposed to use it, if she's not here.

ANNIE: Under the, circumstances, reckon it'll be okay.

> ANNIE *reaches out to touch a cutlet.* KATHLEEN *slaps her hand—a 'don't touch'.*

Ow!

KATHLEEN: It's not midnight yet.

> ANNIE *looks at the cutlets—still frozen as.*

ANNIE: How long have these been

> ANNIE *stops herself.*

KATHLEEN: There were maggots in the flour. I threw it out.

ANNIE: Is that why you stopped?

> *Beat.*

> KATHLEEN *looks down at the book.*

KATHLEEN: I couldn't remember.

ANNIE: What?

KATHLEEN: The words. When I couldn't sleep, we'd sing it, together, but I couldn't

ANNIE: [*going towards her*] Kat

KATHLEEN: [*hard*] No.

> *Beat.*

> ANNIE *goes to take the recipe folder.* KATHLEEN *puts her hand on it.*

Do you remember it, when you were little? Did he sing it to you?

ANNIE: [*quizzical*] Who?

> KATHLEEN *looks at her.*

KATHLEEN: If you can't sleep, it's good to get up and do something.

ANNIE: Yeah, well I blame the fucking quiet. Shit … shit, sorry. It's a, habit.

Bad Annie

KATHLEEN: From The Big Smoke.

Canapés. You have, canapés.

ANNIE: I think they're pronounced canapes [*pronouncing it wrongly on purpose—a joke*].

KATHLEEN: [*not getting it*] They're not.

They're little savoury things. They're named after a French couch.

ANNIE: [*with a laugh*] Are they?

KATHLEEN: Thought you'd know that, in the city.

ANNIE: *Hey*, I wasn't always from the city.

KATHLEEN: But it's where you're from now, isn't it?

Beat.

ANNIE: It's good to see you looking so good, Kat.

KATHLEEN: I'm in my nightdress, silly.

She now looks at ANNIE *again,* ANNIE *smiles.*

Where are your trousers?

ANNIE *looks down, sees her bare legs, feigns shocked horror. They laugh.*

Mum's right.

ANNIE: About what?

KATHLEEN: You got Dad's legs.

ANNIE *laughs,* KATHLEEN *joins in.*

ANNIE: [*this has been said a million times*] And I got Mum's voice.

KATHLEEN: Not Mum's.

ANNIE: What?

KATHLEEN: Nobody said who was going to make the food for tomorrow.

Mum would always make the food, for things like

ANNIE: Yeah, she would.

KATHLEEN: Because it's important, to put on a good spread.

ANNIE: Somebody will put their hand up to do it.

KATHLEEN: Who? [*Looking pleased*] You?

ANNIE: No.

She laughs.

That would be a terrible fucking

We can ask Patrick, when he wakes up.

KATHLEEN: He's not asleep.

ANNIE: What?

KATHLEEN: Patrick said, he said you might not be coming.

He told me not to get my hopes up.

ANNIE doesn't know what to say to this.

KATHLEEN looks down at the mess on the table.

If they can't go up, where do hopes go, Annie?

Beat.

ANNIE: I don't know.

Beat.

KATHLEEN: I saw her. Saw the back of her head, through the door tonight. But I couldn't smell anything cooking and the light was off, and it was just the wind, blowing the curtain. And then I remembered she wasn't allowed in the kitchen anymore.

ANNIE wants to cry—can't or won't.

Sometimes people leave, they go away and you don't see them anymore.

Beat.

And then sometimes they come back.

ANNIE: Kat, Mum isn't … coming back

KATHLEEN: Don't call me that.

Beat.

And you came back, Annie. Even though Dad said you never bloody would.

ANNIE stares at her.

KATHLEEN stares down at the table, begins humming 'The Whole World Is Dreaming'. It's a lullaby of sorts, it soothes KATHLEEN.

As she sings, ANNIE moves to the table and begins clearing up, putting the cutlets onto a dish, humming along.

A noise punctures the gentle mood, as PATRICK slams the back door. Placing keys on a hook, he half enters.

PATRICK: Hey, Possum.

ANNIE: *Possums.*

PATRICK: [*seeing* ANNIE *now*] Shit.

> *He comes in. He looks slightly wired, perhaps a little drunk. He sees the state of the kitchen.*

Shit.

KATHLEEN: Shouldn't say that word

PATRICK: It is *well* past your bedtime.

KATHLEEN: You said it twice.

PATRICK: [*ignoring her*] What's going on here then?

ANNIE: She was cooking. For tomorrow.

> ANNIE *and* PATRICK *throw each other a look.*

PATRICK: Molly's going to do the food for tomorrow, Kathleen. Nothing fancy

KATHLEEN: We have to put on a proper spread.

PATRICK: Yeah, and we will. We will, I promise. You should go up to bed.

ANNIE: We thought you were up there.

KATHLEEN: I didn't.

> *She giggles.*

He goes out *a lot*, at night, Annie. Sometimes he's out for nearly the *whole* night.

> *Grinning, she covers her mouth.*

ANNIE: Lucky I was here then, to keep an eye on things.

PATRICK: [*motioning to the table*] Yeah, and you did a really great fucking job.

KATHLEEN: Patrick!

> *Beat.*

I was making crumbed cutlets.

PATRICK: God help us all.

KATHLEEN: [*holding up the recipe folder*] From the book.

> PATRICK *sees the book she is holding and lurches to grab it.* KATHLEEN *holds fast.*

ANNIE: Jesus, Patrick

PATRICK: Where did you get / that?

ANNIE: She's just playing.

KATHLEEN: I'm not playing, I was making
PATRICK: [*sharp*] Where did you get it, Kathleen?

> *Beat.*

KATHLEEN: [*like a child*] It was in with Mum's things.
PATRICK: You shouldn't have
KATHLEEN: I was careful.
PATRICK: Give it to me.
ANNIE: Patrick, it's / fine.
PATRICK: [*raising his voice*] Just … *give* it to me.
Now. Please.

> *She hands it over. He takes it, closes it, tight.*

KATHLEEN: Lost my place.

> *She is upset, like a child.*

> *A silence between all three of them.*

I've made a mess.
ANNIE: I'll sort it, Pickle.
KATHLEEN: It's Possum. And the cutlets still need to defrost.
ANNIE: Okay.

> KATHLEEN *goes to leave, then turns back.*

KATHLEEN: Will you leave the light on?
PATRICK: Yeah.

> KATHLEEN *goes over to* ANNIE, *leans in, kisses her.* PATRICK *watches.*

KATHLEEN: [*turning to them both*] I'm not going tomorrow. I've got nothing to wear, not anything clean.
PATRICK: We'll talk about it in the morning, okay?

> KATHLEEN *thinks about this, then nods.*

KATHLEEN: Goodnight.
PATRICK: 'Night.
ANNIE: 'Night, Kathleen.

> KATHLEEN *leaves.*

> PATRICK *begins to clear the table, covering food, putting it in fridge.*

What the fuck was that about?

PATRICK: It's late.
ANNIE: Did you drive in that state?

> *He ignores her and keeps packing away. The book now sits on the table.*

You stink, Patrick, of … booze and God knows / what
PATRICK: Thought I smelt of meat.

> *Beat.*

ANNIE: Where have you been?
PATRICK: You the only one allowed out now?
ANNIE: No, of course
PATRICK: Dad wasn't the only one with soft hands round here, Annie.

> *He waves his hands, provocatively, then he keeps clearing.*

ANNIE: Kat said to leave that out.
PATRICK: It's cactus. And we've got rats.

> ANNIE *jumps a little, unnerved, suddenly aware of her bare feet.*

'S what happens, you leave food out on the floor, night after night.
ANNIE: She sounds like Mum. Kat says things … does things, like Mum.
PATRICK: Far as you remember.
She doesn't like being called Kat anymore.
ANNIE: She should be there tomorrow, for the funeral
PATRICK: We'll talk about it in the morning.
ANNIE: I can't sleep.
PATRICK: And I can hardly keep my eyes open.
ANNIE: People deal with grief in different ways.

> PATRICK *looks at her, anger in it.*

> *A sheep, far off, bleats.*

> *He keeps clearing the table. She watches him a moment, comforted, then sits on the table.*

Remember when we used to sneak off down to the shearing shed, at night?
PATRICK: No. I remember going down there to be alone, or with Molly's lads.
ANNIE: I used to watch you all, share a smoke, like it was … the best thing in the world
PATRICK: We all smoked then.

ANNIE: I didn't.

PATRICK: You were ten.

ANNIE: Then we'd jump off the rafters, onto the soft oily wool. Pretend it was snow.

PATRICK: How would we know what snow looked like?

ANNIE: And afterwards, you'd always get the blame, from Dad.

Then you stopped, going there.

PATRICK: Dad knew you were following me. We'd all come back stinking of it, lanolin and tar, and blood, fill our beds with it. He told me if I went down there at night again, I'd live to regret it.

ANNIE: He didn't mean

PATRICK: Yes he did.

That wool would have been weeks of work, whole lot, no good for sale anymore, ruined by us, thinking we were having fucking fun.

ANNIE: It was fun.

Beat.

Are you … okay, Patrick?

PATRICK: I'm drunk.

Nothing she can say to this.

I been over in the far paddock, most of the night. Checking on the ewes. There was one, she'd got stuck in the fence, was about to give birth, but the thing was only halfway out of her, just its legs. Don't know how long she'd been there, a while from the look of her, the sound.

ANNIE: What did you do?

PATRICK: Only thing I could, pulled the thing out.

ANNIE: Was it alright?

PATRICK: It was dead.

That's one thing they are good at, sheep. They have this uncanny knack of finding new ways to die.

Beat.

ANNIE: She was just trying to help, Patrick.

He picks up the book.

PATRICK: Mum's written stuff down, in here.

ANNIE: In … her recipe folder?

PATRICK: Personal things.

ANNIE: Like what?

> *Beat.*

PATRICK: [*looking at her*] I need to go to bed.

ANNIE: I'm sorry, I'm sorry that I wasn't here.

PATRICK: You didn't miss much.

> Na, that's right, you did, you missed a whole fucking / lot.

ANNIE: Patrick

PATRICK: Mum, starting to piss herself, then shit herself.

> Or when she started thinking she was young, a young girl, waiting for someone to take her away from all this. Or, or she was convinced that someone was stealing her money, her savings, not that we had any savings by then, that was in between her eating sugar and … grass. Going wandering off at night and thinking the sheep were the devil, calling out for her, to take her away from all this. That's why we put the new fence up, wasn't for the sheep.

> She'd have these … bursts, of anger. She attacked Molly, with the corkscrew one night. Molly was bringing round some clean laundry. It was the illness, but … that was … I realise now, it was nearly over then. I fucking wanted it to be.

> *Beat.*

> *She goes to move closer to him.*

ANNIE: I'm

PATRICK: I'm going to bed.

> *He moves to leave.*

ANNIE: The farm's ours, Patrick. It belongs to all of us.

PATRICK: It's too late to pretend you give a shit about what's going on here now, Annie.

> *A moment before he leaves, taking the recipe folder with him.*

> ANNIE *stares down at the ruined table, perhaps beginning to silently cry. She wipes her face, picks at the mess of food, bins the meat that's left. Wipes the table.*

> *Then she goes and picks up the guitar, sits, plucks, plays a little, more of a song now beginning to form—the start of 'Turning of the Day'. She sings a line, a few times, trying it out.*

ANNIE: [*singing to herself*] Tell me tales, of …

She looks for a word, maybe sings the opening a few times.

… sacrifice …

She plucks.

… and … sadness.

She wants to cry, can't. She puts the guitar down.

She goes to the stereo, finds and takes out a cassette, puts it on, quietly, listens to a recording of Patrick singing 'Blue Horizon'.

SONG: 'BLUE HORIZON'

    Naked sun's gonna take its toll
    A day's drivin' to the waterhole
    Halfway there and you can't go back
    Smell the water somewhere down the track.

She listens, intently.

    Cool change will kill the heat
    The crack of thunder will make you weep
    Rumble rises in your bones
    Three thousand turn their heads for home.

    And the blue horizon
    Keeps on breakin' through
    Just as long as you keep on drivin'
    The sun will rise for you.

She leaves the cassette playing, turns the lights off.

She goes to the back door, opens it, moonlight shines in.

She takes a cigarette out of her pocket, lights it, draws in a long breath and blows it out the door.

She listens to the song a moment, then walks out the door, into the night as the song continues.

    Remember before the flood
    Newborn stuck in the mud
    The heavens opened and you cursed it all
    Blessed our children and watched them crawl.

KATHLEEN *comes back into the now-empty kitchen in her nightgown.*

> You came in cryin' when you fell too hard
> I still hear laughter across the yard
> Cursed the sky as you watched them grow—

She goes to the stereo and turns it off mid-song.

She then opens the freezer and sees that the lamb cutlets are gone. She goes to the bin, gets the cutlets out and puts them back on the table, to defrost.

She then takes a piece of bread, thinks about eating it, but instead crumbles some onto the floor.

She turns on the light, takes a look around, and then goes back upstairs.

SCENE THREE

The kitchen. The day before.

The kitchen is empty. A sheep can be heard, bleating.

ANNIE *enters through the back door. She is neat yet unsuitably dressed—somehow urban and clean in a little black dress, slip-on shoes with heels, bright lipstick, hair pulled back. She is dragging a small pristine suitcase and carrying a guitar case. She calls out.*

ANNIE: Hello!

> Is anybody …

And she suddenly knows the place is empty.

She parks her bag and guitar. She looks around, opens the fridge, stares a while. Then she goes and looks out the window.

PATRICK *enters, dressed in a flannelette shirt, jeans and work boots, covered in muck. He sees her, but she doesn't see him at first.*

PATRICK: Alright, city girl.

> *She turns, looks self-conscious, as if caught out.*

When d'you get here?

ANNIE: Just now.

He nods.

PATRICK: I would have come and got ya
ANNIE: I know.
PATRICK: If you'd called

> *Beat.*

ANNIE: I thought you'd be working.
PATRICK: I was, I'm on lunch.

> *He opens the fridge, then closes it.*

How'd you get here, from the
ANNIE: I was, was gonna call a cab.

> *He nods, a possible snort—that's her all over. He grabs a broom, sweeps the kitchen floor.*

Then this guy, comes up to me, at the station. Comes out of nowhere. And he's, he's standing in front of me, like he knows me. And I'm thinking, well … crazed fan, at first, though, I mean round here
PATRICK: Everybody knows you. You're famous, our most famous export.
ANNIE: Then he says, you're Annie, Mary and Frank's youngest, and he says, I'm Lenny, like that should mean … and he asks if I'm heading home. And I say no, I just got here, and he says, he meant *home*, as in, to the farm. So, I told him I was going to get a cab
PATRICK: Even though, you didn't.
ANNIE: He already had my guitar, Patrick, he'd got his car door open, says he's coming this way anyway, and then he's beside me, got me and him in a selfie, before I

He seemed … harmless. Though then he drives, whole way, like a bloody lunatic, four K up the track, in record time. And I'm not sure that was true now, about him coming this way.

> *Floor clean,* PATRICK *stops sweeping.*

PATRICK: … Lenny?
ANNIE: Yeah, don't you remember my first love Lenny, well, first … pash.

Though, that doesn't begin to describe it, what happened, down by the dipping shed, when I was twelve. He'd have been … seventeen, which is illegal, even round here. But apparently it was a highlight for Lenny, who's got his own business now, in glass fitting or, something, and it turns out, Lenny does a bit of Uber driving, round here, for the, kids. Not sure he's really ... an Uber driver, officially, but, well, who is?

PATRICK: I'd forgotten.

ANNIE: What?

PATRICK: How much you talk.

Beat.

ANNIE: Sorry.

PATRICK: Na it's

It's good to see you. Bit of life in the place.

Beat.

You look good.

ANNIE: Thanks.

PATRICK: Bit thin.

ANNIE: Thank you.

Beat.

[*Wiping at the air*] I'd forgotten about the flies, and the heat.

PATRICK: Na, you just got soft.

ANNIE: You look exactly the same.

Beat.

I tried to call

PATRICK: I was driving.

ANNIE: I mean, before.

PATRICK: You're here now.

A moment.

ANNIE: I nearly didn't make it. The train. You know there's only one a day, that stops here, according to the website.

PATRICK: There's a website?

She looks at him, he's joking, she's not amused.

There's two stops here now, they just ... haven't, got round to changing it yet.

ANNIE: Thought for a second, it wasn't going to stop at all.

PATRICK: Wouldn't take it personal.

ANNIE: Well, unless you lived here

PATRICK: I do live here.

He puts the broom down.

Molly said you said you were coming today, so knew you'd be on one of 'em.

ANNIE: I couldn't get through on your mobile. And then the phone just rang out.

PATRICK: Was out in the paddock and the answer machine's off.

People kept calling, leaving messages. Wanting to talk to Mum.

Beat.

ANNIE: That new? The fence outside?

PATRICK: Be new to you, been up a while now.

I'll show you round the place if you like, later.

ANNIE: Okay.

PATRICK: Show you the Jenny Craig Paddock.

She looks at him.

Where we put the fat ones.

She stops, is looking around the place. He's looking at her outfit.

ANNIE: So it's … doing alright then?

The farm?

PATRICK: It's ticking over.

Now it is. I've made a few changes around the place. More than a few. We're running Corriedales now, along with the Merinos, and I got a few blokes working for me, helping run things.

ANNIE: That's, good.

PATRICK: Doubt Dad would agree.

But, I been turning the place into something sustainable.

ANNIE: That's really

PATRICK: Not just wool anymore, but meat. Dad would never let me bring another breed onto the land. But, you got to diversify, if you wanna survive now, and that's what I've done. Place is finally starting to look like it can make a profit again.

ANNIE: That's, great, Patrick.

PATRICK: Means I can take a few days off, and the place'll keep going, without me.

She nods. Neither of them know what to say.

So … you been keeping busy, in the big
ANNIE: Yeah. You know.

He doesn't, or doesn't care to.

PATRICK: Heard you got a new manager.
ANNIE: Management.
PATRICK: Everyone wants a piece of you, eh?
ANNIE: It's not really
I wanted … someone more on board, with the way I'm hoping to, to take my music
PATRICK: Right. I'm not, I haven't really … been keeping up, with your latest
ANNIE: God, you don't need to
PATRICK: Still hear about it though, around town. About you, what you been up to.
Whether I wanna know, or not.

Beat.

ANNIE: I'd like that, for you to show me around. I've missed the place.
PATRICK: Hope you brought some other shoes, what do you think this is, 'Farmer Wants a Fucking Wife'?

Beat.

You've got a bit of … on your top.

She looks down, sees there is dust on her. She dusts herself off, badly.

ANNIE: Great. This is the only black thing I brought.
PATRICK: I'll take your

He goes to take her bag. They touch hands. She looks down at his hands. He takes her bag.

Fuck, what you got in here?
ANNIE: No idea.
Just threw a load of stuff in. What do you pack for your own mother's funeral?

This hangs in the air a moment.

What did you wear?
PATRICK: When?
ANNIE: To Dad's?

PATRICK: Can't remember.

Beat.

ANNIE *looks around the room again, wipes at her face, hot.*

He puts the bag down. He pours her a glass of water—the pipes are noisy and the water cloudy. He holds it out.

ANNIE: Place looks … bigger.

PATRICK: Had a bit of a clear-out.

ANNIE: Thought, places were supposed to look smaller.

PATRICK: Than what?

She takes the water.

ANNIE: It smells the same though. I'd forgotten that smell. And the quiet. Think this must be the quietist place in the world.

PATRICK: Even quieter now.

Beat.

She drinks—it's tank water. She pulls a face.

Tanks are low. Hope you brought some rain with you.

ANNIE: Where's Dylan?

He looks at her.

PATRICK: Thought you knew.

ANNIE: Knew … what?

PATRICK: We had to put him down.

ANNIE: What? When?

PATRICK: Around, the same time … he was going deaf

ANNIE: He was always deaf

PATRICK: Then a snake got him.

She sits down, this is hitting her hard.

ANNIE: But snakes, never got Dylan.

PATRICK: This one did.

I've been training up a new dog, border collie kelpie cross

She looks at him, hurting.

Not the same obviously.

She puts the water down.

ANNIE: Sorry, I'm a bit

PATRICK: Nothing a few days shearing won't fix. Could do with a hand.

She looks like she's going to be sick.

I'm just kidding, Two-Tooth.

ANNIE: Don't call me that.

PATRICK: Wouldn't let you near the place. It's lambing season. So there's a lot of it about.

She looks at him.

Life and death. You hungry?

ANNIE: No.

PATRICK: You still a vego?

ANNIE: Yep.

PATRICK: Righto.

Beat.

ANNIE: The fridge is, it's empty.

PATRICK: Normally I go down the pub, when Kathleen isn't here.

ANNIE: I had something on the train. A rice thing. Pilaf. Raisins in it. I'm regretting it now.

Where is Kathleen?

PATRICK: P is for …

ANNIE: What?

Beat.

PATRICK: Kathleen'll be pleased to see you.

ANNIE: I thought she'd be here

PATRICK: She's out.

ANNIE: Where?

PATRICK: She's up at the hospital.

ANNIE: What?

PATRICK: She's / alright

ANNIE: What's wrong with her?

PATRICK: I said, she's / alright

ANNIE: Why didn't you say before

PATRICK: You just walked in, Annie, slow down.

Beat.

She breathes.

ANNIE: Why is Kathleen at the hospital, Patrick?

PATRICK: You sound like Mum. Sit down a minute. Take your shoes / off.
ANNIE: [*loudly*] Patrick!
PATRICK: Now you sound like Dad.

> *Beat.*

She's up there for tests. They're, assessing her.
ANNIE: For what?
PATRICK: A support worker.

> ANNIE *takes this in, sits down in an armchair.*

They came round a week ago, after, Mum
        Kathleen was, she seemed alright with it.
ANNIE: Has it … been a week?
PATRICK: Yeah.

> ANNIE *nods.*

She's been going to the new centre, been going a while. She gets a lift there and back, van comes for her. She's made some friends. I'm half jealous.
        Though she won't talk about her. Mum. Not even sure Kathleen realises that she's … and me, I keep thinking she's going to walk through the door.
ANNIE: She would if she could, knowing Mum. Tell us what to do next.

> *A moment. They both look as if she might appear, a shudder.*

> *They stay looking.*

Then turn the light on.

> *He looks at her.*

PATRICK: She never turned it off.

> *She looks at him.*

Mum, she always left a light on.
ANNIE: Not sure I've ever been in this kitchen without her here.
PATRICK: You get used to it.
        Actually, you don't.

> *She looks at him.*

ANNIE: I might just … dump this upstairs.

> *She goes to exit—up the stairs to the bedrooms.*

PATRICK: There's been some people coming round, to look at the place.

ANNIE *turns.*

I didn't advertise, just, word of mouth.
It's been an alright year so far, touch wood.

He touches his head.

We've got eight DSE to an acre now.

Beat.

Dry Sheep Equivalent.
Mind you, nobody round here could afford what we'd need to get for it now.

ANNIE: [*taking this in*] Right.

PATRICK: But, it'll be good to know what it's worth.

Beat.

She turns to leave again.

Fancy a drink?

ANNIE *turns back to him.*

Special occasion, not special, but … don't reckon I'll be doing any more work today.

ANNIE: Is there still, still stuff to do?

PATRICK: Always stuff to do round here, Annie.

ANNIE: What I really want is a proper cup of coffee.

He doesn't move.

She goes to the kettle, the kind you put on the stove. She goes to put it on.

PATRICK: Gas bottle's disconnected.

She turns and looks at him.

ANNIE: I will have a drink.

PATRICK *looks relieved, goes to the fridge, opens it up.*

PATRICK: Beer or, actually there's only beer.

He watches her as she locates a step ladder tucked under somewhere, puts it up against the fridge. Climbs up, pokes around a load of medals, cups et cetera, to get a dusty bottle of red wine.

She looks pleased, climbs back down.

ANNIE: Special occasion, calls for special occasion wine. This is serious vintage shit.

PATRICK: It's probably just shit.

ANNIE: It's a proper corkscrew job. Let's crack it

She opens a drawer, knows which one, rummages around for a corkscrew, can't find one.

They must have a bloody … somewhere in here there's gotta be a

PATRICK: Best leave it.

She stops.

Things have moved around a bit. I'll pick you one up, later. Corkscrew. Sell them at the servo now.

He hands her his open beer, gets another for himself. She swigs at it.

A moment of silence.

You can smoke in here if you want.

ANNIE: I'm alright.

PATRICK: Just leave the kitchen door open.

ANNIE: You making the rules, now you're man of the house?

PATRICK: Just saying, make yourself at home.

Beat.

ANNIE: I gave up. For my voice.

PATRICK: Good on ya.

But, if you do fancy one, just leave the door open.

She silences something inside.

ANNIE: So, is there much to pack up?

PATRICK: Done most of it. It's in the shed out the back.

ANNIE: All of it?

PATRICK: Not much left now.

ANNIE: What is left?

PATRICK: Nothing to write home about.

She looks at him.

ANNIE: Is that what Mum wanted?

PATRICK: What?

ANNIE: Her stuff to be … packed away? Because maybe, I mean, did she leave instructions, saying what she wanted to happen to

PATRICK: When did you start giving a shit about what Mum wanted?

A dark moment between them.

ANNIE *goes over to a cupboard, opens it. There's little left inside—a few old cassettes, a stereo. She picks up a cassette, looks at it.*

ANNIE: Glad you haven't packed these away yet.

She goes to put the cassette on, he looks tense.

PATRICK: I'm not sure that's … [working.]

But it does, a recording of Patrick singing 'Blue Horizon' begins to play—the opening verse.

SONG: 'BLUE HORIZON' (extract)

PATRICK'S VOICE: [*singing*] Naked sun's gonna take its toll
A day's drivin' to the waterhole
Halfway there and you can't go back
Smell the water somewhere down the track.

Cool change will kill the heat
The crack of thunder will make you weep—

ANNIE: Is that …?

Is that … you, Patrick, singing?

He comes over, turns it off.

Beat.

PATRICK: I might have a shower.

Molly's popping in, make sure we've got everything we need for tomorrow.

ANNIE: She couldn't stop crying on the phone.

PATRICK: She'll be worse tomorrow. And now all her boys have left.

ANNIE: So it's, at the pub then?

PATRICK: [*nodding*] Molly said we can go as late as we like. [*Raising his beer*] Woo.

ANNIE: Are there, many people coming?

PATRICK: Anyone still around. Molly thought, you might want to sing something.

ANNIE: What?

PATRICK: As you got your guitar

ANNIE: No. I mean, I haven't … prepared anything, so

It should be you, that does, says something, Patrick. If anyone's going to.

They look at each other. They both drink.

A moment. A sheep bleats.

I thought you were Dad before, when you came in.

PATRICK: This is his shirt.

ANNIE: Suits you.

PATRICK: Not sure that's a compliment.

ANNIE: It was always Dad. On the platform, at the end, the only one in the sun. He'd never look up until I got right up to him, then he'd just take my bag from me. And I was always … shocked, by how soft his hands were.

PATRICK: Be the lanolin.

ANNIE: Why is the gas disconnected?

PATRICK: Mum kept leaving it on.

Lucky nobody struck a fucking match.

ANNIE: Why didn't you call me, Patrick?

PATRICK: Molly said she'd do it.

ANNIE: I mean, the night Mum …

PATRICK: And say what? It was over then, for her anyway.

ANNIE: I didn't know

That it would take her that fast, the …

She can't say it.

PATRICK: Dementia. D, is for dementia.

Beat.

ANNIE: Who was with her, when she, when Mum

PATRICK: Kathleen was there. We were there together.

ANNIE: That's good, I'm glad.

PATRICK: Was after that, they suggested Kat go up for tests. They said she should have had them years ago, been properly … assessed. Looked at me, like I should have … I offered to go with her. But, Kat said, she wanted to go on her own.

ANNIE: Maybe, maybe a support worker's a good idea. I mean, if it's what Kat wants

PATRICK: How would you know?

ANNIE: I'm just saying, maybe

PATRICK: [*anger in this*] He's called Kenny.

ANNIE: … What?

PATRICK: Kenny, *Kenny* not Lenny. Used to be Kenny's Car Windows, then Kenny's Cars, not a bad bloke, trying to make a go of things here.

> *She downs her beer, puts the bottle down, hard.*

ANNIE: I could buy us dinner, at the pub later.

PATRICK: I'm out tonight.

> *Beat.*

ANNIE: I might go up then, get settled.

> *A moment.*

> ANNIE *goes to go upstairs.*

PATRICK: I moved into your room.

> *Beat.*

ANNIE: It's meat. The smell in here, it smells of meat.

> *She wipes as if at imaginary flies, and exits.*

> *He watches the space she's made, then sees she's left her bag behind. He goes over to the stereo, closes the door on it.*

> *The lights fade.*

SCENE FOUR

The pub. A week before.

PATRICK *is on the pub stage, singing 'Song for Mary'. He sings to no-one. We hear whole song.*

SONG: 'SONG FOR MARY'

PATRICK: [*singing*] First time I touched you
Down among the trees
There was fire on the mountain
There was smoke on the breeze
You laughed at me madly
And kissed you just the same

By the dirty old river
We loved in the rain
'I want you' you whispered
I drowned in your eyes
Loved me so sweetly
I still feel you deeply

The little stone soldier
Stands in the rain
You can hear voices callin'
Will you come back again?
Everyone's leaving
Long may they roam
But she still leaves the light on at home

Letterbox by the roadside
The jet stream above
God knows this dust bowl
Needs a little love
The crows cry in rhythm
Why don't you pick up the phone?
The dogs are goin' crazy
Are you sleeping alone?
Poppies on the avenue
Lest we forget
The power of forgiveness
Is not over yet

Little stone soldier
Stands in the rain
You can hear voices callin'
Will you come back again?
Long may they wander
Long may they roam
But she still leaves her light on at home.

KATHLEEN *enters halfway through the song. She stands out of sight, watching* PATRICK. *She is in her nightdress, drenched from the rain, from head to foot.* PATRICK *keeps singing.*

Bellbirds keep singing
Tryin' to hold back the dry
The dust driftin' sideways
Under a perilous sky
The sheep are needing water
And the town needs relief
Truck in salvation
Truck in some belief

Here's one for trouble
For suffering an' strife
And one for the dirty business
Of getting on with life.

PATRICK *now notices* KATHLEEN. *He stops. She is standing, staring ahead.*

PATRICK: [*spoken*] Kat?

Beat.

KATHLEEN: It's Kathleen.

He puts the guitar down. Looks at her.

PATRICK: What you doing here?
KATHLEEN: That's Dad's.

Now he sees she is wet.

PATRICK: [*gently*] What?
KATHLEEN: Dad's song, for Mum.
PATRICK: I know
     I was just
KATHLEEN: Sad.

Beat.

PATRICK: What you doing here, in your
KATHLEEN: Can I have a drink?

He comes off the stage, goes to her.

PATRICK: Why don't we go home, Possum?
KATHLEEN: I don't want to.

He goes to get closer to her, but she backs away, almost in a trance. He stops, looks at her.

PATRICK: You're in your nightdress, Kat. You must be cold.
KATHLEEN: I'm not.

>*Beat.*

Mum is.
PATRICK: What?
KATHLEEN: I went into her room. She wasn't in her bed.
PATRICK: Shit
KATHLEEN: I couldn't find her at first. But then I did. I found her.
>She was out by one of the fences, the one farest from the house, at the edge, she'd fallen, she was on the ground.
PATRICK: Kat
KATHLEEN: I thought she was sleeping, but her eyes are open. And she isn't sleeping.

>*Beat.*

PATRICK: It's alright, it's alright now.

>PATRICK *attempts to hold her, maybe puts something over her shoulders.*

It's gonna be alright, Kat.
KATHLEEN: It's Kathleen!

>*She looks unsteady, and he holds her, just as she is about to collapse. She struggles a moment, then falls into his arms. He holds her, strokes her head. She is silent and still now.*

END OF ACT ONE

ACT TWO

SCENE ONE

The pub. 1975.

The new TV in the pub has been replaced by an older larger model on the back bar, and the banners, ads and sports posters have been changed, to reflect the year. Otherwise the space is very much the same, in feel.

FRANK is standing on the pub stage, with an acoustic guitar. MARY is standing on a chair, trying to get the faulty TV to work, ignoring him as he strums, sings. She wears the same dress that Annie wore at the start of Act One.

The TV comes in and out, as it broadcasts Gough Whitlam's dismissal— the speech he made in front of a rowdy crowd.

FRANK sings two verses of 'Silver Lining'. The pub is otherwise empty.

SONG: 'SILVER LINING'

FRANK: [*singing*] Feral dogs and fences
       Wedged tail on the wire
       Dark bird in the empty sky
       Carcass on the fire

       Shelter in the doorway
       Rattle of the rabbit gun
       Blowin' seeds of emptiness
       Smokin' in the sun

       There's a fair noose on my shoulder
       Baby, don't hang me out to dry …

He stops, strums, waits.

       [*Singing again*] Baby, don't hang me out to dry …

Beat.

[*Spoken to* MARY] That'd be your cue.

MARY ignores him, as the TV begins working for a second and comes on.

Whitlam's voice on the TV: '... Well may we say, "God save the Queen" ... because nothing will save the governor-general ...'

On the TV the crowd laugh and jeer—the TV cuts out again. MARY bangs it.

FRANK: Mare, that's where you come / in.

MARY: [*without looking at him*] Don't call me that.

The TV comes back on.

Whitlam's voice: '... was countersigned by Malcolm Fraser ...'

Then it cuts out again. MARY groans in frustration.

FRANK: Everybody's waitin'.

MARY: There's no-one here, Frank, 'cept you, *still*. And can't you see, I'm

FRANK: Playing hard to get.

He grins, strums.

She bashes the TV.

I know you're shy, but I can't do it without you, song won't work.

MARY: Then, then it won't work. Like everything else in this ... / dustbowl

FRANK: It already does work, Mare

MARY: Leaving us, in the ... [*wanting to swear*] dark.

FRANK: Now I've added in those lines we wrote

MARY: I didn't write them

FRANK: It's gonna be a classic.

He strums again, the same chord—her cue.

She bangs the TV. It comes back on.

Whitlam's voice: '... undoubtedly go down in Australian history on Remembrance Day 1975, as Kerr's ...'

The TV dies, it stops making any sound at all. MARY stares at it, then realising that it's dead, gets down off the chair.

She stands a moment, staring, hands on hips, aware of the significance of what she's just heard.

You pissed off because you've gone off the smokes?

He strums the chord again.

MARY: Stop that, will you?! You're driving me mad with it.

FRANK: Thought you liked it.

MARY: You, the heat and the … world, falling / apart.

FRANK: You said you liked it, other night, down by the trees.
Said you loved it.

MARY: I'm gonna have that blo— [*stopping herself swearing*] song in my head, for the rest of the night now.

FRANK: See, it's catchy.
And wouldn't be so bad, would it? Worse things to have in your mind at night.

He strums.

MARY: He's gone, Frank, didn't you … Whitlam has gone

FRANK: Good riddance.

MARY: He was the first Australian prime minister to … to visit China, to try and actually … do something

FRANK: By cutting our subsidies and / our

MARY: To make us feel like we could all, be something.

FRANK: What, worse off?

MARY: He's gone, Frank! Thrown out like some dog, doesn't that mean anything to you?

FRANK: And, it's not just a song, Mare. It's a *duet*.

Giving up, she starts cleaning the bar—the end-of-the-evening shutdown.

MARY: Same thing.

FRANK: No, no there's a whole world of difference, Mary. A duet has two parts.

MARY: Not always.

FRANK: Two … halves, that, work in a contrary motion, and then come together as one, in perfect unison.

She stops, looks at him.

MARY: Sometimes, they sing separately, Frank.

He looks at her and her back at him.

FRANK: Well, this one, won't work as a solo, it needs you.

Beat.

MARY: I got ashtrays to clean.

FRANK: I love it when you talk dirty.

[*Into the mic*] Sorry, folks, my missus got a bit of stage fright

MARY: I'm not your missus.

FRANK: What are you then?

MARY: I'm … closing up, as everything's broken, and there's nobody here. You've frightened them all off, with your endless … *duets*.

FRANK: And you've already cleaned that ashtray, twice.

She breathes, puts the ashtray on the bar. He strums.

I know you want to hear it, sing it, so why you fighting it? Face the music, Mare.

He smiles. She breathes.

MARY: You think you're funny?

FRANK: I think you're beautiful.

Because, you are

MARY: You're not even drunk.

FRANK: That a problem? 'Cause plenty fellas round here … saw Les in earlier, giving you the eye.

MARY: He was buying a drink, as this is a pub

FRANK: And wanting more than that.

MARY: You talk in … clichés.

FRANK: They call them clichés, for a reason, Mare.

MARY: You don't even know what that means.

He doesn't.

You know, when I first met you, I thought you were a quiet bloke

FRANK: I was.

He grins.

MARY: Thought you were keen on Molly

FRANK: That was just a, was never gonna come to anything

MARY: And now you come in here every night, talking, torturing me to bloody

She stops. FRANK *looks pleased.*

FRANK: Did you just swear, Mary O'Leary?

MARY: Only because you drove me to it.

FRANK: [*into the mic*] Excuse my missus's language, folks, it's her nerves

MARY: I'm not … And who are you *talking to*?!

Beat.

FRANK: I'm practising. For the future.

MARY: You're a good man, Frank, decent, but you're … you work on a farm and you think you're a rock star.

FRANK: Na, more country.

He grins.

MARY: What use are those songs gonna be on the farm?

FRANK: You. I'm talking to you, Mary. Because, you make me feel … there's a light comes out of you

MARY: Not tonight there isn't.

FRANK: And better than talking to no-one. First sign of madness that, you know

MARY: That and talking to sheep. And I seen you do that too.

FRANK: Only because I was missing you.

MARY *stops, looks at him.*

Though I'm fond of the fluffy little buggers, and I do like a slow roasted shank

MARY: Frank

FRANK: The ewes, ain't you, Mare. Mary.

He smiles at his own joke.

And I don't just work on a farm. It's my farm. One day, it'll be our farm.

MARY: Frank, Frank, I'm glad you've written a new song

FRANK: We wrote it together.

MARY: It's late and it's been a long day, and I'm … tired and
Everyone's gone home, to wait for the heat to break, and I don't blame them.

FRANK: I sing to them, sometimes, to the sheep. And they get this look on their faces, if it's a good song, a sorta cross-eyed look, blissful. Because sheep, Mare, they have poor eyesight, but they are blessed, with excellent hearing. That's a fact.

MARY: And I'll be closing up, any minute.

FRANK: I still got a beer going, and I'm a paying customer

MARY: You didn't pay for that.

FRANK: I can't leave halfway through a duet, Mary.

Because the thing about a harmony, is, it's usually above or below the melody.

And, I always used to write the below bit, see. That's the bit I sing, the bit that comes natural to me. But recently, I'm writing the above bit. Because the prettiest sound, is when the harmony, is a third above the melody, and that's what I hear now. It's your voice, Mary, that's what I have in my head.

Beat. No response.

Do you want me to go?

MARY: [*sharply*] What do you think?

Beat.

FRANK: Okay. Only one thing for it. They won't like it, [*pointing to an imaginary crowd*] but …

He strums and then begins to sing the chorus of 'Silver Lining' by himself, perhaps badly, or just theatrically.

He gets a few lines in, and MARY *can no longer bear it. She marches up onto the stage and stands beside him at the microphone, or grabs it. They continue together.*

She sings the chorus with him, quietly at first, to get it over with, then growing in confidence, but she isn't a natural.

SONG: 'SILVER LINING' (continued)

FRANK: [*singing*] Give me one last kiss
    Give me one more try
    Give me one more shot at the silver lining

FRANK and MARY: See the dust storm coming
    Thunder in the haze
    Feel it in my broken hands
    Fill these hollow days

    Fly on to your loving
    Fly on through the night

First time I laid eyes on you you were
Dancing in the light

This land keeps getting older
Thunder head is hanging in the sky
Give me one last kiss
Give me one more try …

Halfway through the final chorus, she stops, and he sings the last line alone.

FRANK: Give me one more shot at the silver lining.
[*Spoken*] There, told you, it's already a classic.

MARY *drops the microphone, hands it to* FRANK *and steps off the stage, seemingly in a rush.*

[*Calling out to her*] Mare, come on, you gotta admit, it works!
I'm gonna put your name in the

MARY *rushes into the toilet, the door swinging shut.*

FRANK *waits a moment and then steps off the stage. He goes to the toilet door, leans and listens at it a moment.*

Mare?

Beat.

You alright?

He stands back a moment. Then nears it again.

Beat.

You having a secret smoke?
I don't / mind.
MARY: *Go away!*

Beat.

FRANK: What's wrong?
MARY: Can I just have a bit of private, Frank? *Please.*
FRANK: There's no-one here, but
MARY: You're making a scene.
FRANK: To who?
MARY: I asked you to go.

She sounds upset.

FRANK: Yeah, but I knew you were only playing.

MARY: I'm not— [*Her voice breaking*] Why didn't you just ... / go

FRANK: What is it, Mare, tell me?

> *He looks worried. He opens the door a bit, a moment. She goes to shut it, but he stands firm, a crack in the door, strong. Perhaps they can now see each other, but she doesn't come out.*

You sick?

Smells of ... you been

MARY: I'm pregnant.

> *Beat.*

FRANK: What?

Are you? You mean, like ... now / you're

MARY: Yes, Frank, now. I'm pregnant now.

FRANK: Fucking hell.

Sorry. But, fucking hell, Mare, / that's

MARY: Don't, / just

FRANK: That's ... fucking brilliant.

> *Beat.*

MARY: How is it?

FRANK: It's ... it's bloody magical

MARY: It's a mistake.

> *He doesn't know what to say for a moment, his whole world is upside down.*

FRANK: You're in shock. You've just found out you're having a baby, *we're* having a ... woo!

> *She looks at him, something like shame.*

How long you known?

MARY: Few ... weeks, maybe.

FRANK: When were you gonna tell me?

> *Beat.*

When were you gonna tell me, Mare?

MARY: When did you start calling me that? When did I say it was okay for you to ...

He reaches in, or steps in, somehow taking hold of her, an arm or something, it's not threatening, but is strong. Or maybe he just pushes his way into the toilet, so they're face to face.

You shouldn't be in here, Frank. Smells.

FRANK: Got nothing on the men's.

Beat.

I know you're frightened

MARY: You have no idea what I'm thinking … / feeling

FRANK: Okay, so this is sooner than we planned, but it is what we planned, right? Because, it's all I've ever wanted, you, to be my wife. It's the only thing I've

MARY: You can't know that.

FRANK: I do.

Beat.

MARY: What if I had other plans?

FRANK: We'll do them together.

MARY: What about the farm?

FRANK: You'll be a natural.

Beat.

MARY: I'm not ready for this, Frank.

FRANK: I don't understand

MARY: No, you don't.

Beat.

FRANK: Is this about, you being a feminist?

MARY: Frank, it's … I wanna do things.

FRANK: Okay

MARY: I can't do them here.

FRANK: Why not?

MARY: I work in a bloody pub.

FRANK: Best bloody pub in town.

MARY: It's the only pub in town, Frank, and I … I want, more than this. Out there, in the world, something more. I'm going to, change things.

FRANK: I know, because you're brilliant.

MARY: I've been saving.
FRANK: What for?

> *Beat.*

Look, I wasn't gonna say this, Mare, but, I've put the farm in your name
MARY: What?
FRANK: Half of it. So it's ours now, it's *our* / farm.
MARY: Frank … that's not
FRANK: It was always gonna be ours
MARY: No, I don't
FRANK: One day.
MARY: I don't want to stay here, Frank, I … can't, stay, in this place
FRANK: 'Course you / can
MARY: I'll suffocate!
FRANK: *Mary!* What are you talking / about
MARY: I don't want to die here, Frank!

> *Beat.*

FRANK: Mary
> I love you.
MARY: I know.
FRANK: Some people would be bloody happy with that.
MARY: I know. But this wasn't supposed to
FRANK: Don't … *fucking say that!*

> *Beat.*

MARY: I'm pregnant and, and we're not married, Frank
FRANK: Then let's make it right.

> *Beat.*

MARY: It's already wrong, for me.
FRANK: Then what the bloody hell have we been doing?!

> *She is either crying, or on the verge, as is he.*

Don't … cry, please don't
> It'll be alright.

> *Beat.*

MARY: It's still early.

FRANK: What do you

She can't say it, she looks at him.

MARY: It's my body, my decision
FRANK: No it fucking isn't!

He pushes further in and grabs her.

MARY: Get off *me*!

For a second he doesn't, then he lets go, lets her loose. She is crying and he sees it.

FRANK: Oh God, God … I'm … Did I hurt you … hurt the / baby
MARY: Just get out, Frank!

He does.

The door swings closed, he waits by it, as if listening.

Some silence.

FRANK: You smell that?

Rain.

Been waiting for it to rain, for weeks. Sheep always drop their lambs when it rains.

Should see the little buggers, when they come out, Mary, one, sometimes two, at a time. They can do it on their own, but I feel better if I'm there, to make sure they're in the best position for the little ones, to come out.

When they do, Mary, it's like the most natural thing, but it's … like a miracle too. The mother checks them out and then, she licks the little one clean, licks their face, their little nose and mouth, ears, licks them into life.

And they try and stand up then, on their new legs, they're shaky at first, it's hard for them, hard to watch sometimes, but the mother, she stays with them, sometimes for hours, nuzzling in, nose to nose, coaxing them and their little legs, telling them it's alright, to stand up on their own, because she'll be there, as they take their first steps, out in the world.

Beat.

MARY *opens the door and stands looking at him.*

Mary. Mary had a little lamb.

MARY: I don't care about sheep.

FRANK: You just need to spend a bit of time with them, understand how they / think

MARY: I don't want to know anything about them.

FRANK: Contrary to popular belief, you know sheep have an excellent long-term memory

MARY: Shut up, shut up about fucking sheep, Frank.

FRANK: Mind your language, Mare. Mary.

> *He reaches a hand out and touches her stomach tenderly.*

I'll write her a lullaby. Soon as she's old enough to hear it. Before that.

> MARY *looks at him, scared.*

I love you.
> And you love me.
> How could there be anything wrong with that?
> Marry me, Mary O'Leary. Be my wife.

> *She doesn't give him an answer, but stays standing there, as they both look at each other.*

> *The lights fade.*

SCENE TWO

The farm kitchen. Dusk.

KATHLEEN *enters through the open back door in her nightdress, her hands covered in earth. She stares ahead a moment, then she sings the opening to 'The Whole World Is Dreaming'.*

KATHLEEN: [*singing quietly*] Sleep,
> Sleep now my—

> *She stops.*

> *A silence.*

> *Then she bleats, like a sheep, a baby one, uncannily like one.*

> *Another silence, as quiet as the grave.*

> *A moment, then she exits back out the back door.*

SCENE THREE

The pub. The present. Almost sunset.

PATRICK *exits out of the pub, with a beer, clearing up. He dumps a pile of cheap paper plates into an old fire drum outside the door. He checks his phone, no messages. Puts it in his pocket. He looks up at the sky, the stars just becoming visible.*

He is a little drunk. He breathes the wide night air a moment, feels a drop of rain, and heads inside.

He swigs at his beer, goes onto the stage, picks up the guitar, gets the feel of it.

He looks out, like his father, to an imaginary crowd, another life, begins to sing 'Everything I Could'.

SONG: 'EVERYTHING I COULD'

PATRICK: [*singing*] Thunderstorm is passing
    Windows rattle in the wind
    Took the dogs out searching
    Time to bring the stragglers in

    We walk the road for hours
    To keep the emptiness at bay
    I can't escape the feeling
    Never thought I'd see the day

    But I still see her smiling
    When I drink more than I should
    To conjure love out of nothing
    I gave it everything I could

    Who knows what she was thinking
    On that dark and foggy night?
    We were too busy drinkin'
    When she walked into the light
    Now every day is different
    I can't untwist the chain
    Every dream I look to her
    Every night's the same

Still I keep the young ones moving
Until it's too dark to see
I turn to look if she's standing there
Waiting just for me

I swear we made love out of nothing
Makin' more of it than I should
Maybe I'm too old for thinkin'
I did everything I could
But I can still see her smiling
When I drink more than I should
To conjure love out of nothing
I gave it everything I could.

On the last line, ANNIE *enters. She looks somehow wild, windswept, wet from rain. She is barefoot, with muddied feet and carrying her shoes. She's still wearing the vintage dress.*

ANNIE: [*spoken*] She's gone.

PATRICK: … Who?

ANNIE: Kathleen, she's not at the house

PATRICK: [*putting down his guitar*] What do you / mean?

ANNIE: Molly thought she was in bed, but when she went to check on her, she wasn't there.

He comes down off the stage, growing frantic.

PATRICK: Shit. Shit, I have to / go

ANNIE: Molly's staying at the farm, so there's someone there. Les has gone looking around the property

PATRICK: [*pacing*] That should be me!

ANNIE: Molly said best that we stay here, in case Kat comes here.

He stops.

Why would she come here, Patrick?

Beat.

PATRICK: What were you doing there? Thought you'd left, again.

ANNIE: I went to say goodbye to Kat.

PATRICK: In an Uber?

ANNIE: Why would Kat come here, Patrick, she never

PATRICK: You'd have to ask her.

ANNIE: I walked back, walked here, from, but I didn't see her.

PATRICK: Which way did you go?

ANNIE: I started on the road, then I cut across the fields, like we used to

PATRICK: Nobody goes that way anymore.

> *Beat.*

ANNIE: There was a sheep. In a field, a way out. It looked lost.

> Aren't sheep meant to stay in

PATRICK: Not always. They follow the flock, from birth, instinct, and because there's safety in numbers.

> But sheep are easily spooked. They'll run from whatever it is, that frightened them. And that means, sometimes they end up lost.

> They rarely survive out there, alone.

> *Beat.*

I should go / and

ANNIE: We should stay here and wait for her. Molly said she probably hasn't gone far.

PATRICK: What else did *Molly* say?

ANNIE: She said that Dad used to sing here, at the pub.

> *Beat.*

I thought that was Mum. It was Mum that sang here.

> PATRICK *goes to the window, peers out,* ANNIE *goes to get up.*

Is it ... [her?]

PATRICK: Just the wind.

> ANNIE *goes to the bar and sits, considers a beer.*

[*Jittery*] How long we supposed to fucking wait here?

ANNIE: Until she comes back.

PATRICK: What if, something / happens

ANNIE: What else can we do?

PATRICK: She's a ... fucking child, Annie!

ANNIE: No she isn't.

> *Beat.*

> *He grabs another beer.*

She takes one now, opens it, doesn't drink.

They sit a moment.

Raining out there now. Getting dark. I'd forgotten how, it looks, when the sun's almost ... sky's turning ... red, but there's still this ... perfect blue ...

PATRICK: ... Horizon.

They look at each other.

ANNIE: When did you start singing?

PATRICK: What?

ANNIE: When did you start, writing songs?

PATRICK: Can't remember. After you'd left.

Beat.

ANNIE: Did you know Dad sang here?

PATRICK: He'd stopped, by the time you were old enough to remember it.

ANNIE: Most things had, round here, by then.

She drinks now, trying to find courage.

I think we should talk about it, about selling the farm.

PATRICK: What, now?

ANNIE: If you're planning to sell

PATRICK: Kathleen's fucking missing, Annie!

ANNIE: The three of us should talk about it, when she's

PATRICK: She could be hurt!

ANNIE: She'll be ... fine

PATRICK: I don't need your permission, to do anything

ANNIE: No, that's / not

PATRICK: And you don't get to come back for a few days and have a say in what happens here now!

Beat.

ANNIE: I know how hard you've worked, Patrick.

PATRICK: No, you don't.

ANNIE: I'm still a part of this family

PATRICK: Just us two left now.

ANNIE: What about Kathleen?

PATRICK: I meant, Kathleen and me.

ANNIE: This is still where I'm from.

PATRICK: And you couldn't get out fast enough.

ANNIE: There was nothing and no-one left here, not of my own age.

PATRICK: What about Kenny?

Na, sorry, he was older, you / said.

ANNIE: He was nice to me. When I was twelve, Kenny was nice to me.

PATRICK: Yeah, sounds like it.

ANNIE: Everyone here was … older than me, and Kathleen was … I was lonely.

PATRICK: We were all lonely, Annie.

ANNIE: You never seemed it.

PATRICK: You were too young to know what was going on.

ANNIE: That's not a crime.

PATRICK: Na, just a fact.

ANNIE: I was just a kid when I left. But, you

PATRICK: I stayed, I stayed behind.

ANNIE: You belonged.

PATRICK: That what you told yourself, is it?

ANNIE: You were my older brother, my hero.

He laughs, bitter.

You never came to the phone, when I called.

PATRICK: I was *working*.

ANNIE: You were always a part of the farm. You were wanted.

PATRICK: I was needed.

Beat.

ANNIE: Mum never wanted me.

PATRICK: Oh, poor bloody Annie

ANNIE: I wrote to her, every week when I first left. I told her all about my life. She never wrote back. I don't even know if she read my letters.

I didn't know how to make her love me.

Except when I sang.

PATRICK: Everybody loved you then.

ANNIE: I sang for her, Patrick, because I thought that's what she wanted

PATRICK: And you loved being the centre of attention

ANNIE: No, I didn't.

PATRICK: What about the night of Dad's funeral? You got everyone's attention then.

ANNIE: And after I'd sung my heart out, Mum wouldn't even look at me.

PATRICK: So you left. For The *Big Smoke*.

ANNIE: Stop, calling it that

PATRICK: Left us all behind, for your dream of a big new life. The one, that got away.

ANNIE: I didn't *get away*, I was, pushed! Mum fucking pushed, drove me away!

> *Pause.*

PATRICK: We came to see you once.

ANNIE: What?

PATRICK: Me, and Kathleen, came to the city.

ANNIE: When?

PATRICK: Year or so ago, must have been. Mum was, she was getting bad, and Kathleen, she kept asking about you, and I didn't know what to tell her.

I googled you. You had a gig on, in the city, headline act, that weekend. So I, I drove us down. Wouldn't have if I'd known about the fucking parking, but we got there just in time, just as the guy before you finished. He was good

ANNIE: Where was this?

PATRICK: Big place, was packed, I was impressed, and we waited. Kathleen was beside herself, couldn't sit still. And then after a while, this other guy comes on, announces, that you wouldn't be coming, singing, that night. Apologised, to us all. Was only then I realised I didn't know where you lived.

ANNIE: You should have called

PATRICK: Wasn't even sure I had your number. And Kathleen was starving by then, with all the excitement.

I took her to this Moroccan place, just down the road from the venue. All dark lighting, no chairs, you had to sit on these cushions on the floor. But the food was, delicious. Kat goes right ahead and orders a chermoula, lamb fucking chermoula. [*Laughing at the memory*] We ate like kings, two of us, on the floor.

ANNIE: You could have … tried to

PATRICK: Was too late, by then.

ANNIE: I bet you'd had enough of the city.

PATRICK: Na, I was just getting started. But Kathleen, she was dead on her feet.

ANNIE: [*nodding*] I'd have liked to have seen you.

PATRICK: Me too. Those tickets cost me twenty-five bucks a piece.

>*Beat.*

So what was it?

ANNIE: It's not the same, having to … sing, in front of all of those people, who've paid to see you, it's not the same as singing round the table, after tea.

PATRICK: Na, I meant, why d'you bother coming back, we were doing fine without ya, and I was finally enjoying a quiet fucking drink.

ANNIE: [*at breaking point, shouting*] I just lost *my mother too*!

>*She does something physical, perhaps throws or smashes something?*

>*Pause.*

PATRICK: You wore a little black dress, to Dad's funeral.

Something you didn't get from round here. Everyone said you were just like Mum that day. Then you sang, and everybody cried. Then Mum took Kathleen home.

ANNIE: In case there was a scene.

PATRICK: Na, I don't think it was that.

ANNIE: Then she picked a fight with me. She told me she never wanted to see me again. And I left, without saying goodbye, so she couldn't see me cry.

>*She wipes at her face.*

I don't even know how he, how Dad died. Nobody told me.

>*She looks at him.*

>*A moment.*

PATRICK: They said it was the drought that killed him. But it was almost over, we were through the worst, could have recovered, but Dad, he'd had a gutful.

And turns out, he was wrong about me.

>*Beat.*

I'm good at it, Annie, this place. Managing people, the land, turns out.

ANNIE: Then why are you selling it? You said it was doing well

PATRICK: I said it was ticking over. Be three years before it's anything like being near to being clear and that's if the drought doesn't make it here. Then we'll be fucked.

Beat.

ANNIE: Maybe I could help.

He looks at her.

I've got a bit of money put aside. Not much, but

PATRICK: We need more than that.

ANNIE: The farm was, everything to Mum and Dad, it was their life, we have to keep it.

PATRICK: You mean *I* have to keep it.

Beat.

He grabs another beer, drinks, this is painful.

He goes out one morning, Dad, 'cross the paddock, to where you can't see from the house, and he finds them. Mob of Merinos, fifty of them, stuck in the dam, and he loved his Merinos, but they're not known for their intellect.

Half are them are already dead. Rest of them are stuck there, struggling, can't get out. And he knows he'll get stuck in the mud too, he goes in to help them, won't be able to get them out, they're too far in. So he goes and gets his gun. And he shoots them, one by one, till they're dead, lucky for them he was a good shot. That's thirty wool producers, at a hundred and twenty a head, gone, in one morning, and then he goes back to work. One of the shearers found him, two days later, in the front of the ute, heart just, stopped. And he hated that fucking ute.

ANNIE: I'm sorry

PATRICK: You left, Annie, you made a *choice*!

She steps towards him, he backs away.

D is for dead-end town

ANNIE: Patrick

PATRICK: D is for daughter who didn't come back for five fucking years.

ANNIE: I had to go

PATRICK: To see your own mother, who was disappearing, dying

ANNIE: I was frightened

PATRICK: Who was the living fucking dead

ANNIE: Of getting stuck here!

PATRICK: Or for me, Annie, me, what about *me*?!

Beat.

ANNIE: I couldn't stay, I'm sorry.

PATRICK: And I couldn't leave.

Pause.

ANNIE: Please don't sell the farm. It's all I've got, of them.

PATRICK: They're gone.

ANNIE: It's all I've got.

PATRICK: What about your big career?

ANNIE: I can't sing anymore.

He looks at her.

I've stopped, being able to, sing, in front of … anyone. I open my mouth, and words come out, but I can't hear what I sound like. And when I do, hear myself, it sounds … wrong. I can't … feel anything.

My manager, he let me go, because I couldn't … I had all these gigs lined up.

The new … manager, they're much smaller, not even … they said maybe I should try writing my own stuff. But I can't, I've got nothing to say. I'm empty, lost.

Except I'm terrified. I realise now I always was terrified.

Beat.

He drinks.

A moment.

PATRICK: Dad left the place to Mum, and she gave it to me. She didn't want to. But in the end she didn't have a choice.

She told me to sell it.

ANNIE: What?

PATRICK: Mum told me to sell the farm, before she died.

ANNIE: She didn't know what she was saying.

PATRICK: Yes she did.

Beat.

But I can't sell it, can I?

I can't leave Kathleen, where would she fucking go?

ANNIE: You don't know what she wants.

PATRICK: [*hard*] And you do?

> *She looks at him, so much pain between them, but finally coming out.*

ANNIE: [*quietly, almost in a whisper*] What's in it, the, the recipe book?

> *He drinks, so does she.*

PATRICK: I was hoping for … news of Dad being a, a secret Mason, or a … repressed homosexual, or the tiniest sniff of her, of Mum, having an affair, with Les, at least, in there.

It's full of clippings.

ANNIE: Of … what?

PATRICK: She cut out a picture of you from the paper, on that march you led.

ANNIE: I didn't … It was a protest.

PATRICK: Against the evils of the meat trade.

ANNIE: I got arrested for that.

PATRICK: Dad had a good laugh.

ANNIE: [*hurt*] About me being arrested?

PATRICK: About you being a vegetarian. Mum said, it was, a phase, to piss him off.

ANNIE: Yeah … / well

PATRICK: She wrote about you. Every week she'd, Mum'd write something about you, your life, filled every page with the stuff. It was like, she was writing it for you. But, she was writing it for her.

ANNIE: I don't … understand

PATRICK: Your borrowed fucking futon and your singing lessons. The traffic and trams, that kept you awake. And the hard water, you couldn't get used to, and that you were homesick, that all you wanted to do, was come home, at first. But you'd stay, until you got something, till you'd achieved, something.

> *She looks at him, eyes filled with tears.*

ANNIE: I didn't …

> *She can't speak.*

PATRICK: Your letters are in there. Worn out, from reading.

ANNIE: [*crying now*] I didn't know

PATRICK: You were all she talked about at the end. Even though you'd gone. Kept asking me to sing to her and then, then I realised, she thought I was Dad. So I did, I sang to her. She was better then, for a bit.

> *Beat.*

ANNIE: You were the one they got right, Patrick.

PATRICK: And you were the one they set free.

> *Beat as this lands.*

ANNIE: [*quietly, afraid*] What about you?
What did she write in there, about you?

PATRICK: Nothing. There's nothing about me in there. Not one word.
She wrote about Kathleen being born, life, up until she realised that Kathleen was

> *He stops, swigs, finishes the beer.*

Then she stopped, writing about us. And Dad, he stopped singing.

> *Beat.*

It was him, him that sang, Annie, not her.

ANNIE: But she told us, it was her, that she gave it up, for

PATRICK: It was always him.

> *He grabs another beer.*

And now his songs are mine.

> *Beat.*

> ANNIE *takes his beer off him, goes to have a swig and then, whilst he watches, pours it away in the sink.*

> *She sits, seems to settle, for the first time all night, exhausted.*

> KATHLEEN *enters, unseen by them. She stands in the doorway, watching them, she is holding the recipe book.*

She wanted to be a sheep.
Kathleen told Mum and Dad that, at the dinner table, over a roast. She was eight years old. I was four and I remember it, like it was … She puts down her knife and fork and announces that she wished she'd been born a baby lamb, free.

He laughs, it's sad.

Dad didn't miss a beat, just drank his beer and ate the rest of his dinner in silence. Me … I was, in awe of her. Then Mum says, they're not free, Kat, lambs are not free, not ever.

KATHLEEN: I thought you'd gone.

PATRICK: [*hugely relieved*] Kat …

KATHLEEN: It's Kathleen.

PATRICK: Where you

> *He now sees she is holding the recipe book, her hands stained with earth.*

How did you get here, Possum?

KATHLEEN: I drove.

PATRICK: What?

KATHLEEN: I drove Dad's truck.

ANNIE: Since when, since when did you drive?

KATHLEEN: Dad used to let me have a go on it. Round the farm.
When Mum wasn't looking.

> PATRICK *goes to the window.*

PATRICK: [*looking out*] Shit, where's the bloody

> KATHLEEN *comes into the room. There is some blood on her head. It's not a serious wound and looks more dramatic than it is, but she's slightly disorientated.*

> ANNIE *goes to her.*

KATHLEEN: Don't get / angry

PATRICK: Where's the fucking truck?

KATHLEEN: I knew you'd / get

ANNIE: Nobody's … angry with you, Kat, but just, tell us where the truck is.

KATHLEEN: Where it came to a stop.
Under the stars.

> PATRICK *now looks over and sees that she is bleeding. She's still clutching the book.*

ANNIE: What happened to your head?

KATHLEEN: [*she seems unsteady*] Not … sure

PATRICK: [*going to her too now*] Shit, are you, is she … alright, fuck

ANNIE: Don't make a scene.

> *Beat.*

How many fingers am I holding up?

> *She holds up three fingers to* KATHLEEN.

KATHLEEN: Five.
But I can only see three, because you're hiding the other two. Not very well.

> *Beat.*

ANNIE: [*smiling*] I think she's probably okay.

> ANNIE *dabs at* KATHLEEN*'s head with a napkin from the bar.*

KATHLEEN: Dad never taught me how to stop, the truck. He would always do that bit.

> PATRICK *has now come over to look at her head, touches it. She winces.*

PATRICK: What were you thinking?
KATHLEEN: That you'd *gone*!

> *Beat.*

ANNIE: She's okay, Patrick.
KATHLEEN: I'm okay.

> KATHLEEN *smiles at her.*

> ANNIE *wets the napkin, cleans the blood off, it's a small scratch.*

ANNIE: No bones broken.

> KATHLEEN *shakes her head.*

[*Smiling*] See if I can find a bandaid.
PATRICK: I'm taking her home.
KATHLEEN: Can't I stay? For a bit?
Annie?

> ANNIE *looks to* PATRICK.

I *am* the oldest.

> ANNIE *laughs, more relief than anything else. Goes looking for first-aid box behind the bar.*

ANNIE: Ask your brother.

> KATHLEEN *looks at him—he's relieved.*

PATRICK: Okay, but, just for a bit.

> KATHLEEN *grins.*

> ANNIE *locates a first-aid box, brings it around and dresses* KATHLEEN*'s head.*

KATHLEEN: I drove slow, like Dad taught me.

PATRICK: Good, that's, good.

KATHLEEN: I miss Dad, teaching me stuff. And I saw the Southern Cross.

PATRICK: Did ya?

KATHLEEN: You can see it, if you face south and find the two brightest stars, in the Milky Way

PATRICK: That's

KATHLEEN: I hadn't finished.

> Beta Centauri and Alpha Centauri, they're the pointers, and if you draw a line from them and go up a bit, there's the Southern Cross.

ANNIE: Did Dad teach you that too?

KATHLEEN: No, Mum did.

> *Beat.*

> ANNIE *finishes up her head, with a clean bandaid.*

ANNIE: You'll live.

> *A pause between them.*

> ANNIE *pinches her nose,* KATHLEEN *giggles,* PATRICK *watches.*

KATHLEEN: I thought you'd gone, Annie.

PATRICK: She had. Twice.

KATHLEEN: Then she came back.

> I've never had a drink in here.

> ANNIE *looks at* PATRICK*, realising in this moment that this is true.*

ANNIE: [*going behind the bar*] What can I get you, madam?

KATHLEEN: I'm a ms.

ANNIE: Right. Anything, anything you want.

KATHLEEN: I haven't got my purse.

ANNIE: I won't tell if you don't.

Beat.

KATHLEEN: Can I have a Coke. Full fat?

ANNIE: A bottle of our finest full fat Coke coming up, Ms Kathleen.

KATHLEEN *grins.*

ANNIE *locates a bottle of Coke, opens it up, puts it on the bar.*

KATHLEEN *puts down the book, on the bar, both see this. She picks up the Coke.*

KATHLEEN: Quiet at the house. Couldn't even hear the sheep. Are they gone too?

PATRICK: Na, they're just, sleeping. They've had a busy few weeks, earned a rest. And you know, Possum, sheep only sleep when they feel safe.

KATHLEEN: Like Mum.

Both look at her now. PATRICK *goes to her, to touch her—they are all feeling this.*

PATRICK: I'm sorry, that I wasn't … That night, that I left you alone, Kat. Kathleen.

KATHLEEN: I wasn't alone.

ANNIE: She had three thousand sheep to keep her company.

ANNIE *smiles at* KATHLEEN.

KATHLEEN: Annie couldn't sleep with the noise, Patrick, when she first went to the big smoke, and now she can't sleep here, with all the quiet.

ANNIE: Actually, I slept like a baby last night, when I went back to bed, for the first time in, I don't know how long.

KATHLEEN *looks at the book.*

KATHLEEN: Why did Mum do things she didn't want?

PATRICK: What?

KATHLEEN: Why did she cook lamb all the time? In all those different ways?

PATRICK: She didn't … have a choice.

KATHLEEN: But why would she cook it every day, for two years, if it made her sick?

ANNIE *looks at* PATRICK.

PATRICK: That was 2006.

    Dad had to, buy in feed, because of the drought, crated feed round on the ute.

KATHLEEN: The porridge truck?

PATRICK: Yeah. So, we had to eat whatever was left.

KATHLEEN: The two-tooth?

PATRICK: Yeah.

KATHLEEN: Two-tooth stew.

ANNIE: I remember that.

PATRICK: Could have been worse.

ANNIE: Not much.

KATHLEEN: The youngest ones, had two little baby teeth.

ANNIE: And then every year they'd get another two.

KATHLEEN: Until they were full mouths.

PATRICK: Yeah.

KATHLEEN: And then broken mouths.

    Another moment, heavy between them.

PATRICK: And Dad loved every one of them the same.

KATHLEEN: Yes, but sheep are born and raised for different things.

    Beat.

Some are raised for breeding. Some are kept to look after the land. Merinos, are bred for their wool, the young lamb's wool's the best, the finest, softest, the first shearing. So they're prized, above the others

PATRICK: / Kat

KATHLEEN: And some are raised for their meat. You shouldn't get too close to those, the store lambs, they're born in July and sold in December, that's why they're called The Terminals. Because, they have nothing to look forward to.

    Beat.

Am I ill because of Mum?

PATRICK: What?

KATHLEEN: Because she didn't want me?

PATRICK: No, *no* of course / not

KATHLEEN: Did Mum do something, to make me ill?

PATRICK: Mum would never have done

KATHLEEN: But why did she keep me, if she didn't want me?

A heavy beat—it's painful.

ANNIE: She did, Kat, she *did* want you … she did, she just, wanted other things too.

KATHLEEN: That's not our fault.

ANNIE: No, it isn't.

KATHLEEN: How were we supposed to know what she wanted, if she never told us?

Beat.

ANNIE: She was just trying to protect you.

KATHLEEN: But she was still unhappy.

Beat.

ANNIE: She did it for us. Mum, tried to make life better, for us.

KATHLEEN: But, it was still lamb.

KATHLEEN *picks up the book.*

A silence as all acknowledge its presence, weight.

I wish Dad had seen you sing.

ANNIE: He did.

KATHLEEN: Not you, Patrick.

Patrick sings all the time now, Annie.

ANNIE: Does he?

KATHLEEN: Mostly Dad's songs. He found them in the shed, written down. He sings to himself mostly, and he hasn't got any of his own songs yet.

ANNIE: Songs don't … they don't belong to people, Kat, not one person.

KATHLEEN: Why?

ANNIE: Because, they belong to everyone, anyone, who sings them.

Beat.

KATHLEEN: What about Dad's songs, for Mum? She used to like it when he sang.

But then, he stopped.

PATRICK: The songs weren't just for Mum.

PATRICK *walks over, picks up the guitar. He plays the intro to 'The Whole World is Dreaming'.*

He is about to sing, but ANNIE *now sings the first verse, having listened and learned it.*

PATRICK *looks up, a little startled, but realising that it feels right. He keeps playing as* ANNIE *sings.*

SONG: 'THE WHOLE WORLD IS DREAMING'

ANNIE: [*singing*] Sleep, sleep now, my love
        There's nothing to fear
        I'm right here beside you
        Fly, fly through the night
        The stars in the window
        Are flying above you

        Little eyes that shine in the dark
        Creatures alive in your heart
        Angels will come
        To carry you home
        You're never alone
        When the whole world is dreaming.

PATRICK *now joins in the song and they continue together.*

ANNIE and PATRICK: Hear the wind in the trees
        Night birds are calling
        A love song to guide you
        High, high on a cloud
        The desert is waiting
        Her arms will find you.

Perhaps KATHLEEN *joins in the last verse, even if just to hum, or sing quietly, now remembering.*

        And I … I'll still be here
        Little baby, there's nothing to fear
        Angels will come
        To carry you home
        You're never alone
        When the whole world is dreaming.

ANNIE *is speechless at the end of the song, choked up.*

All three of them let the song settle, somehow more together now, than they have ever been.

A moment.

KATHLEEN: Are you leaving now, Annie?

ANNIE: No.

KATHLEEN: But you've got your bag.

ANNIE: Not … yet.

KATHLEEN: Is it because Patrick took your room?

ANNIE: No.

KATHLEEN: He doesn't even like it.

ANNIE: What?

PATRICK: I preferred it up the front.

ANNIE: So do I, now.

> PATRICK *looks at her. She smiles.*

KATHLEEN: Can I have some chips? I wasn't hungry before, but I am now.

PATRICK: That's, good.

> *He grabs a bag of chips, chucks them at her.*

> KATHLEEN *eats her chips for a bit as they watch.*

KATHLEEN: Why don't they have lamb-flavoured chips?
They have all kinds of other meat flavours, beef, chicken. Bacon, but no lamb?

PATRICK: She's got a point.

> ANNIE *smiles, grabs a chip.*

ANNIE: What kind of lamb-flavour chips would work, do you think?
What kind of … lamb dish, because, there's a lot to choose from.

> KATHLEEN *thinks hard a moment.*

A, is for

> *They both look at* ANNIE.

A, is, for
A …

KATHLEEN: Aussie rissoles!

> KATHLEEN *grins.*

ANNIE: That could work. In a … bistro kinda way. Aussie rissole chips
KATHLEEN: B, is for
ANNIE: Burger! A good old *lamb burger.*
PATRICK: Steady on vego
ANNIE: C, C is for

Beat.

[*To* PATRICK] Come on, country boy, C, C is for
PATRICK: Curry, no, no, couscous, lamb couscous,
ANNIE: D
PATRICK: No, no I already said, I told you.
ANNIE: I know
PATRICK: D doesn't have a
ANNIE: I know what you said, and I
KATHLEEN: Dhansak.

Both look at KATHLEEN

Lamb dhansak. We have it up at the centre.

Sometimes I help them make it, help mix up the spices, from scratch. There's a few spices in it, but it's mild, because it's sweet as well, so most people like it, even if they don't like spicy food, it's an all-rounder.

I prefer the spicier curries, but I'm learning to cook all kinds, sometimes I stay late and cook for the people that stay over. They have their own rooms there, bunk beds, TV room, and they said I was a natural and I think I probably am.

They've said there's always a room for me there, if I want. I like cooking. But I'm not sure about bunk beds.

Beat.

Molly snores, like a train. Worse than Dad.
PATRICK: Would you … would you like to, have a room there, Kathleen?

Beat.

KATHLEEN: Maybe.

Just for a few nights a week maybe.
PATRICK: Okay.
KATHLEEN: At the start.

Beat.

PATRICK: Okay.

KATHLEEN: They've said I can start next week, if I want.

She finishes her Coke.

A moment between them—a sense of change in the air.

KATHLEEN *begins to hum 'The Whole World is Dreaming'. They watch her. She stops.*

Can I have another Coke?

ANNIE: I think one's enough.

KATHLEEN: But / I

ANNIE: You'll never sleep otherwise.

KATHLEEN *seems to accept this.*

ANNIE *reaches out and straightens* KATHLEEN*'s hair with a hand, as if born to do it.* PATRICK *watches.*

A moment.

How would you feel, Kathleen, if, if Patrick went away?

PATRICK: Annie

ANNIE: Just for a bit.

ANNIE *looks at* PATRICK.

KATHLEEN: With you, you mean?

ANNIE: No.

KATHLEEN: Where? Where are you going, Patrick?

Beat.

PATRICK: Dunno.

KATHLEEN: [*thinking*] When I'm up at the centre, you mean?

Beat.

PATRICK: Yeah.

KATHLEEN: What about the sheep?

ANNIE: Thing is, we were thinking

PATRICK: What were we thinking?

ANNIE: That I might keep an eye on it, the farm. For a bit.

PATRICK *looks at her.*

KATHLEEN: You don't know anything about the farm, Annie.

PATRICK: Once more, she's got a point.

ANNIE: You need to get with the times, Paddy, female farmers are on the rise.

PATRICK: Yeah, that'd be females that know something about farming.

ANNIE: I've got a, rough idea.

He laughs.

I saw enough of it, growing up. And, I could learn, it's in my blood. And I like sheep.

KATHLEEN: You're a vegetarian.

ANNIE: I'd need a bit of help obviously.

PATRICK: [*with a snort*] More than a bit.

ANNIE: You said yourself, Patrick, with the new staff, things could, tick over

PATRICK: For a while

ANNIE: Without you. That's what you said.

Beat.

I wouldn't have your way with people, not at first.

Not, ever.

KATHLEEN: You can't have a natural way with people, and sheep.

ANNIE: You've got to diversify, Patrick, for things to grow.

Keep growing.

Beat.

KATHLEEN: [*working it out*] So, you'd be at the farm, when I come home, Annie?

ANNIE: Yeah. We'd be there together.

If that's

KATHLEEN: Okay.

Beat.

KATHLEEN *hands* ANNIE *the recipe book. She burps.*

Pardon me.

ANNIE *and* PATRICK *smile, like kids.*

We should throw it out.

KATHLEEN *is looking at the book.*

We've got other things to cook now, so we don't need it anymore, and it's private.

Beat.

A moment between them as the three look at each other.

ANNIE: Kat

KATHLEEN: Don't call me that, she's gone now.

A moment between them.

KATHLEEN *gets down off her stool and she walks towards the door, opens it—she's leaving.*

PATRICK *and* ANNIE *look at each other.*

PATRICK: [*calling to her*] Kat!

KATHLEEN: [*without looking back*] Can still see them. The stars. Bright.

KATHLEEN *exits.*

Beat.

PATRICK: I'll … go, and …

ANNIE *nods.* PATRICK *heads for the door.*

ANNIE: [*calling out*] Maybe have a look at the truck, Patrick! Because I don't fancy walking home again tonight, not in those shoes.

PATRICK *turns and looks at her, acknowledges what she has said. He smiles and then exits. He stands at the door a moment, looks out into the night, can't see Kathleen, or anyone. He walks off into the night, after her.*

ANNIE *puts her shoes back on, smiles to herself and sits down at the bar, by the recipe book. A moment before she opens it, about to read, then thinks against it and closes it.*

She picks up the guitar, and slowly begins to find a song—'The Turning of the Day'. Picking through it, finding it, line by line, and then singing the beginning. She sings it beautifully.

SONG: 'THE TURNING OF THE DAY' (Annie's version)

ANNIE: [*singing*] Tell me tales of memory and madness
Roaring in my sleep and in your mind
I'll reach out to cover you in gladness
For we must leave our innocence behind

> All along the frontier we have plundered
> The trail of thickest blood won't fade away
> Out across the dark red earth we've wandered
> Until we reached the turning of the day.

ANNIE *gets up, pleased, wanting to share the song. She goes to the door, looks out.*

▼ ▼ ▼ ▼ ▼ ▼ ▼ ▼ ▼

PATRICK, *now* FRANK, *appears, in front of her—he has been waiting.*

FRANK: Mary.

ANNIE *as* MARY *starts, not expecting anyone to be there.*

MARY: Jesus! You gave me the fright of my
FRANK: Sorry.

Beat.

It's Frank.
I'm … Frank.
MARY: I know.
FRANK: Yeah? [*Looking pleased*] That's, good.
MARY: What you doing out here?
FRANK: Waiting.
MARY: For what?

Beat.

FRANK: Where you going?
MARY: Home.
FRANK: Why?
MARY: Shift's finished.
FRANK: You not having a knock-off? You were dancing, just before
MARY: [*shaking her head*] Not tonight.
FRANK: Something I said?
MARY: You didn't say anything. You just sat there, the whole night, at the bar, not saying anything.
FRANK: That a crime?
MARY: No. Just a fact, Frank.

She rummages in her handbag, getting ready to leave, swears to herself under her breath.

FRANK: I meant to … I wanted to … sing you something. A song.

MARY: Yeah? Then what?

She continues to rummage in her bag, distracted.

FRANK: You could … join in, sing along. I wrote it for

MARY: [*amused*] I don't sing.

FRANK: Everybody sings.

MARY: Not me, Frank.

FRANK: How d'ya know, if you've never tried it?

MARY: [*looking up from her bag*] You got a light, Frank?

He hasn't, but he likes her saying his name. He hesitates, as if he might have, she gets nearer.

FRANK: Na, sorry.

She tuts. Then, remembering something, she comes back towards him, looks under the drum, finds a box of matches.

She looks pleased, gets a cigarette out of her bag. She stands close.

You on tomorrow?

MARY: No.

FRANK: What about the day after?

MARY *shakes her head, puts her cigarette in her mouth, but doesn't light it.*

When's your next shift?

MARY: I'm going away, for a while.

FRANK *nods, his whole world collapsing.*

FRANK: Where … to?

MARY: The city.

FRANK: Why?

MARY: [*smiling as she thinks about whether to tell him*] I'm going on a march, next week.

It's a, an anti-nuclear rally … about the effects of uranium mining now, because of … Rum Jungle.

It's not just about us anymore, Frank, it's about the effects on the whole planet. It's gonna be huge, people are really fired up.

He stares at her, unsure what to say. He nods, she is obviously fired up, excited.

I'm ... going with these friends, they've got a room free in their house, so I'm going to stay with them, see what I

FRANK: You should be careful

MARY: Of ... what?

FRANK: Just, careful.

She smiles, laughs a little.

What?

MARY: You.

She smiles. He looks grave.

I've said I'll come back.

FRANK: When?

MARY: To work through the summer, until they find someone else at the pub, for my shifts, and to get enough for a plane fare.

FRANK: To where?

MARY: Whole world out there, Frank.

She grins.

FRANK: You gonna light that?

She puts the cigarette in her mouth.

I meant the fire. Freezing my nuts off here.

She looks at him. He smiles, and she sees for the first time how handsome he is.

MARY: Last drinks. You should go in.

FRANK: Why would I do that?

He holds out his hand to her. She looks at it, unsure what it means.

He takes the matches from her hands, they touch, a spark.

He lights a match, then lights the fire, expertly—it takes.

Shouldn't smoke anyway. Woman with your looks.

MARY: Bit sexist, Frank.

FRANK: Na. Just a fact.

He smiles, she does, perhaps both are at the fire, so neither sees the other.

MARY: Beautiful fucking night.

He elbows her—it's familiar somehow and he's in heaven at being this close and in contact.

FRANK: Mind your language.

Both look at the fire a moment. She holds the cigarette, doesn't smoke it, breathes the air.

You won't get sky, nights like this, in the big *smoke*, you know.
MARY: I'll take my chances.

Beat as they watch the fire, close.

FRANK: So, you wanna hear it then?

She looks at him.

This song.
MARY: Maybe.

But not tonight.

They stay looking at the fire, under the stars, standing close now, as the lights fade.

THE END

RED STITCH

THE ACTORS' THEATRE

playwriting australia

presents

Lamb

A new play with songs

13 NOVEMBER–16 DECEMBER 2018

Playwright
Jane Bodie

Director
Julian Meyrick

Songwriter
Mark Seymour

Set and Costume Designer
Greg Clarke

Lighting Designer
Efterpi Soropos

Sound Designer/VCA Secondee
Justin Gardam

Stage Manager
Alysha Watt

Assistant Stage Manager
Zsuzsa Gaynor Mihaly

Patrick/Frank – **Simon Maiden**

Annie/Mary – **Brigid Gallacher**

Kathleen – **Emily Goddard**

This play was developed through Red Stitch's INK writing program in partnership with Playwriting Australia through their Ignition program. We thank: the Cybec Foundation, Lyngala Foundation, Malcolm Robertson Foundation, City of Port Phillip, Copyright Australia, and the Seaborn, Broughton and Walford Foundation.

RED STITCH | THE ACTORS' THEATRE

Artistic Director
Ella Caldwell

General Manager
Fiona Symonds

Development Manager
Angelica Clunes

Front of House Manager
Hannah Bullen

Production Manager
Greg Clarke

Production Trainee
Millie Spencer

RED STITCH ENSEMBLE

Ella Caldwell	Olga Makeeva
Richard Cawthorne	Dion Mills
Kate Cole	Christina O'Neill
Brett Cousins	Joe Petruzzi
Erin Dewar	Dushan Philips
Ngaire Dawn Fair	Tim Potter
Casey Filips	Ben Prendergast
Daniel Frederikson	Tim Ross
Emily Goddard	Clare Springett
Laura Gordon	Kat Stewart
Kevin Hofbauer	Sarah Sutherland
Justin Hosking	Andrea Swifte
Rory Kelly	David Whiteley
Caroline Lee	Harvey Zielinski

Rear 2 Chapel Street, St Kilda East, VIC 3183
http://redstitch.net/ | FB: @RedStitchTheatre | T: @redstitch

boxoffice@redstitch.net | 03 9533 8083

RED STITCH ACTORS' THEATRE

As Australia's leading actors' ensemble, Red Stitch puts artists at the centre of its practice. Established in 2002, we play a vital role in the development and presentation of new Australian works through our unique INK playwriting program. With a national reputation for the quality of our work, Red Stitch remains at the forefront of contemporary Australian theatre practice, and we offer opportunities for theatre-makers at all stages of their careers to hone and develop their craft.

www.redstitch.net

playwriting
australia

PLAYWRITING AUSTRALIA

Playwriting Australia is the national new play development company. We seek, develop and champion outstanding new Australian stories by unique playwrights that will inspire present and future generations. We connect talent with opportunity, bringing playwrights together with other theatre artists and companies to create an expanding repertoire of new plays and productions. We push to extend art, ambition, quality and diversity of playwrights and playwriting.

www.pwa.org.au

DIRECTOR'S NOTE

The simplest truths are often the hardest to talk about. Getting older involves complex changes to our minds and bodies. Things look different because they are different. Strength, health, flexibility, adaptability, quick hands and quick wits: these things are revealed for what they are—impermanent gifts, liable to diminishment if not disappearance with the passing of time.

Mortality is that most terrifying type of philosophical construct, 'a condition'. Aka it can't be changed. It is what is, whatever it is. And in respect of aging, it affects us all, no exceptions. The difference is how we respond to it individually.

Lamb's central character isn't present for the first hour of the play. Mary was a farmer's wife, mother of two daughters and a son, who have gathered back at the family home for her funeral and an unearthing of the secrets of the past.

Except there aren't any really. Lamb eschews rote melodrama for the long, sad complex, reality check that accompanies profound bereavement. In her last years, Mary had Alzheimer's, and it is perhaps no coincidence that both Jane's mother and my own also have this disease. Not quite a tragedy, yet not quite anything else, Alzheimer's rubs out a person by inches, taking now one memory, now another, leaving family and friends struggling to know what to say to the sufferer when words no longer refer to the things they should.

As Lamb's action unfolds, the life that was Mary's is brought into vivid relief, not least in Act II, when the play steps back in time to show the early courtship of her husband, Frank. It's a marriage impossible to judge, either then or later. As Frank is a farmer, Mary marries the farm as much as she marries him, and this reality—the reality of sheep, mud, drought, work, and more work—is her life from the moment she takes him up. In the play, it's clear it's a choice she had grave doubts about, collapsing her hopes of a freedom beyond her small rural town irrevocably. Perhaps less clearly, but hanging in the air like smoke after a bushfire, is the suggestion that Frank would have liked another kind of life too. But it is what it is, whatever it is.

The dialogue of Lamb is written by Jane Bodie, the songs and lyrics by Mark Seymour. Yet the play overall is the result of a deep creative partnership, and some of the events in the play reflect Mark's experience, while some of the songs reflect Jane's impulses. It is a great thing to have great songs in a great play. They carry the story into a new dimension of 'sensuous particularity', to borrow a phrase of Schiller's.

Functionally, they act a bit like soliloquies, opening up inner vistas of feeling normally impenetrable to realist drama. They have the quality of vivid dreams, haunting the mind with hints of a world that can never be fully disclosed. A big thank you to Mushroom Records for allowing the song lyrics to appear in the printed version of the play. They are as integral a part of it as the spoken words.

Kathleen, Patrick and Annie are, in many ways, children like any others: trapped in a rerun of their parents lives unless they can find a means of transcending them.

For it is not enough to 'reject' our families. 'Rejection' just sees us making their mistakes all over again. The past is never past, but sits on our shoulder, judging us, and failing us. To escape it requires more than a negative reaction, more than running away. It requires a re-engagement with the original problem, and the search for a new solution. In other words, an act of courage and imagination.

Lamb is about that act of courage and imagination for Mary's three children. It isn't easy. Fear, anger, confusion, jealousy and grief are very real currents running through their relationships with each other— feelings slow-cooked over years of carefully nurtured resentment and slight. Such emotions don't go away, but have to be managed so that their pernicious effects give way to an affirming understanding that change is possible. Even when it doesn't feel it. In fact, especially when it doesn't feel it.

The tenor and tone of Lamb is hope; hope hard won, but hope nevertheless. Perhaps in a life lived as hard as it is in rural Australia, that sort of hope is the only one going. But it's as real as the farm that Mary and Frank and their children give their lives to looking after. One of the paradoxes of the art form is that drama true to the pain of life helps us cope with it so much better.

Finally, I would like to note that Lamb marks sixteen years of collaboration between Jane and myself as playwright and director, and our third production together. Theatre doesn't usually make the people who do it rich. What it offers instead are imaginative friendships full of surprise, humour, joy and warmth. These are inestimable gifts in a world sometimes heavy with suffering. Words cannot do justice to the gratitude I feel for having known and worked with Jane over such a long time.

Julian Meyrick
Director

JANE BODIE
PLAYWRIGHT

Jane is a playwright, screenwriter, director and mentor. Her plays, including *Savage*, *Music*, *Hinterland*, *This Years' Ashes*, *A Single Act*, *Still*, *Ride* and *Fourplay* have been performed worldwide, from London to Australia. She won the Victorian Premier'S Literary Award in 2006 for *A Single Act* and a Green Room Award in 2003 for *Still*.

Jane has written extensively for TV and radio, including *The Secret Life of Us*, *Crash Burn* and *Moving Wallpaper*. Radio includes *Seeing Somebody* and *In Glass* for Radio National and BBC Radio 4. Her short film *Alice* directed by Garth Davis was selected for screening at Cannes Film Festival. Jane has worked as dramaturg on many standout productions, including Emily Sheehan's *Hell's Canyon*, Katie Beckett's *Which Way Home* and Michelle Lee's *Rice*. She worked at The Royal Court Theatre and at Central School of Speech and Drama as a writing tutor, and was Head of Playwriting at NIDA until 2012. Jane was Associate Artist at The Griffin Theatre in 2013 and Artistic Associate at Playwriting Australia in 2014. In 2015 she was awarded an Arts Victoria Fellowship to create three new works. She is currently writing a play, *Water*, for Black Swan State Theatre Company and is creating a new eight-part TV drama series

JULIAN MEYRICK
DIRECTOR

Julian is Strategic Professor of Creative Arts at Flinders University and Artistic Counsel for the State Theatre Company of South Australia. He was Associate Director and Literary Advisor at Melbourne Theatre Company 2002-07 and Artistic Director of kickhouse theatre 1989-98. He is the director of many award-winning productions, including *Neighbourhood Watch* for the STCSA in 2014 and *Angela's Kitchen*, which won the 2012 Helpmann for Best Australian Work. He was the director of the inaugural production of *Who's Afraid of the Working Class?* and winner of the 1998 Green Room Award for Best Director on the Fringe. Productions include: for Red Stitch Theatre, *The Realistic Joneses*, *Dead Centre/Sea Wall*; for MTC, *Tribes, The Birthday Party, Thom Pain, Enlightenment, The Ghost Writer, A Single Act, Cruel and Tender, Dinner, The Memory of Water, Blue/Orange* and *Frozen*; for STC, *The Vertical Hour, Doubt* and *The Snow Queen*; for Griffin, *Angela's Kitchen* and *October*; for fortyfivedownstairs, *Whiteley's Incredible Blue* and *Do Not Go Gentle...*; for 10 Days on the Island, *As We Forgive*. As a historian he has published books on the Nimrod Theatre and the MTC, and numerous articles on Australian culture and cultural policy. *The Retreat of Our National Drama*, his second Currency House Platform Paper was launched in 2014. He was a founder member and Deputy Chair of PlayWriting Australia 2004-09, and a member of the federal government's Creative Australia Advisory Group 2008-10. He is currently a member of the Currency House editorial committee and the Council for Humanities, Arts and Social Sciences board. His book *Australian Theatre after the New Wave* was published by Brill in 2017. *What Matters? Talking Value in Australian Culture*, co-authored with Robert Phiddian and Tully Barnett, was published in 2018 by Monash University Publishing.

MARK SEYMOUR
SONGWRITER

Mark Seymour is a singer/songwriter best known for his work with Australian band Hunters and Collectors. Mark has been writing and recording songs for over 30 years and is responsible for some of our best-loved anthems. 'Throw your Arms Around Me' is a stand out. Mark has written extensively for theatre and film. Of particular note has been his collaboration with Melbourne director Donna Jackson in political theatre projects such as *We built this City* and *Dust*. These events involved both songs and sound design. He is currently composing material for a new album.

GREG CLARKE
SET AND COSTUME DESIGNER

Greg Clarke is a set and costume designer with 30 years of experience designing for drama, dance and musical theatre. He has worked on a significant number of premier productions including, Melbourne Workers Theatre's *Who's Afraid of the Working Class*, La Boite Theatre's *The White Earth*, *The Narcissist*, *Rio Saki and Other Falling Debris*, *Way Out West*, *Sex Cubed* and *Kitchen Diva*, Umber Production's *Risk*, Accolade Productions' *The Pink Twins*, Queensland Theatre Company's *The Family*, *On the Whipping Side*, *One Woman's Song*, and Playbox Theatre's Inside 2000 season of plays including *Violet Inc.*, *Baby X*, *Elegy*, *So Wet* and *Like A Metaphor*.

EFTERPI SOROPOS
LIGHTING DESIGNER

Efterpi has returned to performing arts lighting design for only the third time in ten years with *Lamb*. She trained as a designer at NIDA, graduating in 1987 and then spent just over 20 years as a performing arts designer, lecturer and creator of several large and small scale public art lighting installations. In 2007 after completing a Masters, Efterpi began a four-year artist-in-residence at Monash Health developing a new community art practice of multi-sensory, de-stress spaces in hospitals and aged-care called Human Rooms. Theatre companies Efterpi has worked with include MTC, Playbox Theatre, Chamber Made Opera, Sydney Theatre Company, Griffin Theatre, Queensland Theatre Company, Black Swan, Melbourne and Sydney festivals, as well as international projects in Edinburgh, London, Hong Kong, Toronto, Vancouver, Ottawa and Washington.

JUSTIN GARDAM
SOUND DESIGNER / VCA SECONDEE

Justin Gardam specialises in sound design, video design, and music composition for theatre. He is a graduate of Monash University's Bachelor of Performing Arts and is currently studying a Master of Dramaturgy at the Victorian College of the Arts (VCA). His recent work includes *The Nose* (Theatre Works/The Bloomshed). Further design credits include *The Market is A Wind-Up Toy* (Theatre Works/The Bloomshed); *Unsolicited Male*, *Ironbound*, and *NK: A Kazantzakian Montage* (Q44 Theatre); *Philtrum* (North of Eight); *Awakening* (fortyfivedownstairs/MUST); *Catherine: the body politic* (La Mama); *F.* (Riot Stage/Poppy Seed), *True West* (Matchstick Theatre), and *Julius Caesar* (Essential Theatre). Justin has assisted on *Suddenly Last Summer*, *Desert 6:29pm, The Moors* (Red Stitch); *Abigail's Party* (MTC); *Merciless Gods* (Griffin/Little Ones Theatre), and *The Lonely Wolf* (MTC NEON/Dirty Pretty Theatre).

ALYSHA WATT
STAGE MANAGER

Alysha is a Melbourne-based stage and production manager in live performance and events. Since graduating from VCA with a Bachelor of Fine Arts in Stage Management in 2017, Alysha has worked with companies such as Zeb Fontaine Theatre, Hit Productions, The Little Theatre Company and Peter Jones Special Events. She continues to pursue fostering meaningful working relationships to enable collaborative creative processes.

ZSUZSA GAYNOR MIHALY
ASSISTANT STAGE MANAGER

Zsuzsa is a second year Bachelor of Fine Arts (Production) student at the Victorian College of the Arts (VCA), majoring in Stage Management. They are a hardworking and driven team player with a passion for collaborative, creative environments. During their time at the VCA, they contributed to such projects as *Mother Courage and her Children* (2017), *The Drowsy Chaperone* (2017), *US28* (2018) and *Peter Pan* (2018). This is their professional debut.

SIMON MAIDEN
PATRICK/FRANK

Simon Maiden has an extensive list of credits since graduating from WAAPA. He has featured in films such as *Romulus, My Father* directed by Richard Roxburgh, the World War II drama *The Great Raid*, *The Killer Elite* and Jocelyn Morehouse's *The Dressmaker*. Simon's most recent feature is the Leigh Whannell directed sci-fi thriller *Upgrade*, with Simon as the voice of 'Stem'. On television, he has been seen in *Newton's Law*, *Wentworth*, *Jack Irish*, *The Doctor Blake Mysteries*, *Winners and Losers*, *City Homicide*, *Rush*, *Satisfaction*, *Tangle*, the tele movies *Hawke*, *Dangerous Remedy*, *Underground: The Julian Assange Story* and the mini-series *Deadline Gallipoli* in the role of Winston Churchill. His numerous theatre credits include the world premiere of *Last Man Standing* for Melbourne Theatre Company, *Robots Vs Art* with Tamarama Rock Surfers, *Ruben Guthrie* for Red Stitch, *Criminology* and *Love* for Malthouse Theatre. He was recently seen in *Curtains* for The Production Company.

BRIGID GALLACHER
ANNIE/MARY

Brigid Gallacher's theatre credits include *Prehistoric* (Elbow Room), *Nightingale and the Rose* (Little Ones Theatre), *Colder* (Red Stitch), *Merciless Gods* (Little Ones Theatre), *Salt* (She Said Theatre), *The Way Out* (Red Stitch), *Dracula* (Little Ones Theatre), *Timeshare* (Malthouse Theatre), *Dangerous Liaisons* (Little Ones Theatre), *Dropped* (La Mama), *Arden V Arden* (Hayloft Project), *Romeo and Juliet* (ZLMDSC), *Tuesday* (MKA), *Circle Mirror Transformation* (MTC), *Baal* (Malthouse/ STC) and *The Nest* (Hayloft Project). Her film and television credits include *Holding the Man*, *Force of Destiny*, *Summer Heights High*, *Underbelly: Tell Them Lucifer Was Here*.

EMILY GODDARD
KATHLEEN

Emily Goddard graduated from Ecole Philippe Gaulier, Paris in 2010, supported by the Ian Potter Cultural Trust and Empire Theatres Bursary. Recent theatre credits include *Noises Off*, *The Boy at The Edge of Everything* and *Elling* (Melbourne Theatre Company), *Angels in America* and *The Lonely Wolf* (Dirty Pretty Theatre), *You Got Older* and *Glory Dazed* (Red Stitch), *Inner Voices* (Old Fitz), *Mess* (The Bush, London/UK National tour, Caroline Horton/China Plate), *The Unspoken Word is Joe* (Brisbane Festival/ MKA), *Moth* (Arena), *The Walls* (Attic/Erratic), *Peer Gynt* (Four Larks) and *Os Pequenos Nadas* (Ultimo Comboio Teatro, Barcelona). Also a theatre maker, Emily is the creator of the critically acclaimed Bouffon anti-bonnet drama *This is Eden* (HotHouse/ fortyfivedownstairs). Her screen credits include *Newton's Law*, *Twentysomething*, *This Week*, *Live*, *Cracks*, *Shyness is Nice* and *The Dating Ring*. Emily has been nominated for three Green Room Awards for Outstanding Female Actor, most recently for *This is Eden*.

This play was developed through Red Stitch's INK writing program in partnership with Playwriting Australia through their Ignition program.

RED STITCH

THE ACTORS' THEATRE

playwriting australia

Red Stitch would like to thank the following supporters who generously contribute to our INK program.

CREATIVE VICTORIA

CITY OF PORT PHILLIP

COPYRIGHT AGENCY CULTURAL FUND

Cybec Foundation

Lyngala Foundation

MALCOLM ROBERTSON FOUNDATION

SBW foundation

Kindred

This project has been assisted by the Australian government through the Department of Communication and the Arts' Catalyst—Australian Arts and Culture Fund.

Australian Government
Catalyst—Australian Arts and Culture Fund

www.ingramcontent.com/pod-product-compliance
Lightning Source LLC
Chambersburg PA
CBHW050018090426
42734CB00021B/3315